JACKSON POLLOCK

The Great American Artists Series

ALBERT P. RYDER *by Lloyd Goodrich*

THOMAS EAKINS *by Fairfield Porter*

WINSLOW HOMER *by Lloyd Goodrich*

WILLEM de KOONING *by Thomas B. Hess*

STUART DAVIS *by E. C. Goossen*

JACKSON POLLOCK *by Frank O'Hara*

IN PREPARATION

JOHN JAMES AUDUBON *by Ruthven Todd*

JOHN MARIN *by Kenneth Sawyer*

BEN SHAHN *by James Thrall Soby*

ARSHILE GORKY *by Harold Rosenberg*

Jackson
POLLOCK

by Frank O'Hara

Distributed by Pocket Books, Inc.

GEORGE BRAZILLER, INC.

NEW YORK 1959

For information address the publisher,
George Braziller, Inc., 215 Fourth Avenue,
New York 3, N.Y.

LIBRARY OF CONGRESS CATALOG CARD NUMBER: 59-12228

PRINTED IN THE UNITED STATES OF AMERICA
BY R. R. DONNELLEY & SONS COMPANY

CONTENTS

TEXT 11
PLATES 33
CHRONOLOGY 113
SELECTED BIBLIOGRAPHY 119
INDEX 123

ACKNOWLEDGMENTS

THROUGH THE YEARS of my acquaintance with Pollock's work I have absorbed, consciously and unconsciously, many of the insights of artists and friends, a debt which is difficult to acknowledge. I would like, however, to thank those whose help in assembling the present material on Pollock and his work, whether through conversation or critical writings, directly or indirectly, has been so great: Mrs. Lee Krasner Pollock, Clement Greenberg, Harold Rosenberg, James Schuyler, Robert Motherwell, Sam Hunter and Thomas B. Hess, to name only a few. It is to Grace Hartigan that I owe an awareness of certain aspects of Pollock's genius, and to Larry Rivers a particular appreciation of the beauties of *Number 29,* 1950.

The brief chronology is based on those prepared by Sam Hunter for the catalog of the exhibition he directed at the Museum of Modern Art and by Clement Greenberg for Evergreen Review. The bibliography is based on material organized by Bernard Karpel, librarian of the Museum of Modern Art, for European catalogs of the exhibition of Pollock's work circulated in Europe by the Museum's International Program.

Our thanks go also to the many public and private collections through whose kind cooperation we have been able to reproduce the works included in this book.

F. O'H.

JACKSON POLLOCK

Photograph by Hans Namuth

Art is full of things that everyone knows about, of generally acknowledged truths. Although everyone is free to use them, the generally accepted principles have to wait a long time before they find an application. A generally acknowledged truth must wait for a rare piece of luck, a piece of luck that smiles upon it only once in a hundred years, before it can find application. Such a piece of luck was Scriabin. Just as Dostoievsky is not only a novelist and just as Blok is not only a poet, so Scriabin is not only a composer, but an occasion for perpetual congratulations, a personified festival and triumph of Russian culture.

PASTERNAK, *I Remember*
(Essai d'Autobiographie)

AND SO IS Jackson Pollock such an occasion for American culture. Like the Russian artists Pasternak mentions, his work was nourished by international roots, but it was created in a nation and in a society which knew, but refused to acknowledge, the truths of which Pasternak speaks.

We note that Pasternak puts these general truths in the plural, for culture is capable of entertaining more than one truth simultaneously in a given era. Few artists, however, are capable of sustaining more than one in the span of their activity, and if they are capable they often are met with the accusation of "no coherent, unifying style," rather than a celebration. Even Picasso has not escaped from this kind of criticism. Such criticism is panoramic and non-specific. It tends to sum up, not divulge. This is a very useful method if the truth is one, but where there is a multiplicity of truths it is delimiting and misleading, most often involving a preference for one truth above another, and thus contributing to the avoidance of cultural acknowledgment.

If there is unity in the total *œuvre* of Pollock, it is formed by a drastic self-knowledge which permeates each of his periods and underlies each change of interest, each search. In considering his work as a whole one finds the ego totally absorbed in the work. By being "in" the specific painting, as he himself put it, he gave himself over to cultural necessities which, in turn, freed him from the external encumbrances which surround art as an occasion of extreme cultural concern, encumbrances external to the act of applying a specific truth to the specific cultural event for which it has been waiting in order to be fully revealed. This is not automatism or self-expression, but insight. Insight, if it is occasional, functions critically; if it is causal, insight functions creatively. It is the latter which is characteristic of Pollock, who was its agent, and whose work is its evidence. This creative insight is the greatest gift an artist can have, and the greatest burden a man can sustain.

The early works

Although Pollock is known as the extreme advocate of non-figurative painting through the enormous publicity which grew up around his "drip" paintings of the late 1940's and early 1950's, the crisis of figurative as opposed to non-figurative art pursued him throughout his life. Unlike his European contemporaries, art for him was not a matter of deciding upon a style and then exploring its possibilities. He explored the possibilities for discovery in himself as an artist, and in doing so he embraced, absorbed and expanded all the materials which he instinctively reached for, and which we later find to be completely pertinent to the work. His method was inclusive: he did not exclude, from one period to another, elements in which he had found a previous meaning of a different nature. Thus it is that we find a relationship, however disparate in meaning, between the forms of the early Untitled, ca.

Drawing. 1938. Ink on paper, 17⅞ x 13⅞″. Collection Lee Krasner Pollock

1936 (plate 3) and the *Moon Vibrations* of 1953 (plate 76), between the Untitled, 1937 (plate 5), which Sidney Janis has pointed to as perhaps the first of the radically "all-over" paintings later to be the preoccupation of a number of his contemporaries, and his own later "all-over" paintings, such as the Untitled of 1950 (plate 47) and the *Frieze* of 1953–55 (owned by Mr. and Mrs. Burton Tremaine, Sr.). So the figurative images of the great black-and-white period of 1951–52 relate to the numerous early drawings in which he changed the idioms of Picasso and André Masson into his own (naturalistic then) conception of space and incident. A good example of what he accomplished in the latter case, where space becomes the field of incident, may be seen in the *White Horizontal,* 1941-47 (plate 12), an accomplishment which Pollock did not dwell on, though the ramifications of what he found in doing it linger in his work and the work of others to this day.

The Mexicans

Pollock, from the first, had quite apparently a flair for drama, in the sense of revelation through stress and conflict. His student period has been so well and thoroughly expounded by Sam Hunter in the preface of the Pollock exhibition he organized for the Museum of Modern Art in 1956, that a detailed retracing of his development would be repetitive.

It is not surprising that Pollock, after experiencing the attempt made by his teacher Thomas Benton toward heroic regional expression, should have become interested in the works of Rivera, Orozco and Siqueiros, which were then very much in the air. By the middle Thirties, Rivera had already painted murals in New York, San Francisco and Detroit, as well as the one for Rockefeller Center which was refused in the face of great publicity because of the portrait of Lenin. By this time Rivera had also delivered his famous dictum that art should express "the new order of things . . . and that the logical place for this art, . . . belonging to the populace, was on the walls of public buildings." Though Pollock was undoubtedly more interested in the works of Orozco and Siqueiros, this statement of Rivera's may have somehow pointed the way to the heroic scale of his early *Mural* (plate 10) and the huge masterpieces of 1950, *Autumn Rhythm* (plate 50), *Number 32* (plate 59) and *One* (plate 51). These are indeed paintings for the populace, as well as for individual pondering.

The drawings and paintings done during the period of Pollock's interest in Orozco and Siqueiros, however, seem to me to be studies of their unabashedly dramatic treatment of subject—it is not art which interested him here, but their attitude toward content, their convictions. American "social-content" paintings of the 1930's and early 1940's seem very tentative by comparison. And Thomas Benton, in introducing El Greco and the Italian Mannerists into the Great Depression, did an unusually interesting thing, no matter how the actual paintings turned out, but it was not a powerful thing.

Surrealism

The influence of Surrealism, though as a movement it provoked few masterpieces, has been considerable and seldom has been given its just due. It is true that the Surrealist periods of Picasso, Miró and others produced great works, but the powerful personalities of these artists, the broad sweep of their creativity, tends to minimize their debt to Surrealism. For American painters, I think, the importance of Surrealism's influence lay in a less direct stimulation. For instance the whole basis of art-consciousness and art-confidence in America was changed by Surrealism, and even if more literary than painterly works influenced American life, the basic findings of the Surrealist struggle toward subliminal meaning has not failed to effect all modern art which is not commercial, and much that is ("the hidden persuaders," for instance).

The basic theory of Surrealism is a far greater liberation from the restrictions of preconceived form than any amount of idiosyncratic experimentation, and it finally destroyed the post-Renaissance vision of visual structure supported by the rationalizations and syllogisms of semi-popular science. That the principles of Surrealism were often expounded in painting by means perversely counter to the genuine accomplishment of Cubism does not negate the fact that Surrealism destroyed, where Cubism only undermined on the same rationalistic basis as before. Cubism was an innovation, Surrealism an evolution. The former dealt with technique, the latter with content. The truths implicit in Surrealism were touched upon and hinted at by Picasso (who did not need them) and Masson (who did), but they had to wait for the works of Pollock, and of such other American artists as Mark Rothko and Clyfford Still, to be acknowledged, to come to life, to speak, to apply. Surrealism enjoined the duty, along with the liberation, of saying what you mean and meaning what you say, above and beyond any fondness for saying or meaning. Max Ernst is to me a "fond" painter. As with those images of the American Indian, of sand-painting, that most natural and fragile of arts, those images of the Western reaches, all of which seem to have haunted his subconscious from time to time, recurring by allusion, the many "influences" which can be traced are less interesting as influences than as materials for Pollock's spirited revaluation. Now that Pollock has touched and clarified them, it is hard to see these materials as he found them. In their quality, which he created by his work and which we find by relating them to him, not by his analogy to them, he has given them reality for us outside his work, as a cultural by-product of his own achievement. This goes, too, for Miró, whose work has been enhanced for us by Pollock.

Arshile Gorky

Gorky, that magnificent painter, provides us with a case of artistic revaluation which contrasts with that of Pollock. For in Gorky pertinent developments of much European art, not only recent, were assimilated for American painting. But it was at the expense of Europe. Gorky, by his peculiar genius for something-of-value, is able to make a certain aspect of Picasso boorish, Miró frivolous, Masson leaden; and even a master like David may seem over-explicit when compared to *The Orators* (now destroyed) or *Diary of a Seducer*. Not so, Pollock, who did not appropriate (as an artist has every right to do—I am simply making a distinction) what was beautiful, frenzied, ugly or candid in others, but enriched it and flung it back to their work, as if it were a re-interpretation for the benefit of all, a clarification and apotheosis which does not destroy the thing seen, whether of nature or art, but preserves it in a pure regard. Very few things, it seems, were assimilated or absorbed by Pollock. They were left intact, and given back. Paint is paint, shells and wire are shells and wire, glass is glass, canvas is canvas. You do not find, in his work, a typewriter becoming a stomach, a sponge becoming a brain.

Male and Female, 1942

His first masterpiece, *Male and Female* (plate 7), was painted when Pollock was thirty and sums up the interests of the preceding years, fluent in imagery, strong in stance; the two protagonists face each other in a welter of cabalistic signs and numbers, and emotional flurries. They are in search of a unifying symbol. This unity is found by Pollock through the confusion of their aims and choices, in the unity of their search, which is mutual. Like Picasso's famous *Girl before a Mirror,* the images reflect each other's sexual characteristics, but now the emphasis is on the love which has occasioned their search. The sexual imagery is extraordinarily complex in that it seems to be the result of the superimposition of the protagonists at different stages of their relationship. They are not double-images in the routine Surrealist sense, but have a multiplicity of attitudes. At different times one sees them facing each other, then both facing in the same direction (to the left), then with their backs to each other but the memory of the confrontation vivid in their appearance. Suggestions of eyes (upper and middle right, left-of-center and lower left) peer at the viewer, as if to guard the lovers without veiling them. Their youth and ambivalence is carried by the brilliance of the color and its almost brutal relevance to the subject.

Since several of the paintings of this period have mythological titles it may not be idle to wonder if perhaps this male and female do not have some allegorical significance. Certainly the painting is not "about" Surrealist or Freudian sexual motivations. It is an expression of classical, resolved violence; one is present at the problem and at the solution simultaneously. The imagery is not privately sensual, but categorically sexual, forensically expounded. The obscurity of the relationship is made utterly clear. The occasion is important and public.

In *The She-Wolf* (plate 13) of the following year, one of six works which bear on the probability of allegory, Lupa, the saving nurse of Romulus and Remus, is advancing with full dugs towards a child whose face appears in the lower left. This is undoubtedly Romulus, for though the wolf nursed both brothers, Romulus later killed Remus. She is not yet giving suck, and Romulus, the stronger, would be first to feed.

That Pollock was deeply interested in the mythology surrounding Romulus and Remus seems fairly certain. To cite only a few instances, we may remember that when Romulus and Remus came to vie for the rule of what was to be Rome, precedence was decided by omens and flights of birds. Remus saw only six vultures, Romulus twelve; therefore Romulus ruled. This may be the subject of *Bird Effort,* 1946. Later Romulus, after killing his brother, was shunned by his neighbors. By establishing a sacred grove as sancutary, he surrounded himself with a number of criminals, fugitives and foreigners (the future citizens of Rome). Deprived of the possibility of intermarriage with the neighboring inhabitants, Romulus established games and feasts in honor of the god Consus, held in great secrecy, to which were borne kidnapped virgins. It is these festivitives, perhaps, that *Guardians of the Secret* (plate 14) is celebrating, a painting which is a marvel of spatial confinement and passionate formalism, formalism brought to the point of Expressionistic defensiveness. If so, the *Wounded Animal* (plate 16) is one of the sacrifices at these Consualia. We are told that during one of these celebrations the rape of the Sabine women took place. As we all know, the Sabines were defeated, but a major disaster was averted by the intervention of the Sabine women, who entreated their parents and husbands to lay down arms. All the Sabines then came to live in Rome, and their king ruled jointly with Romulus. It seems to me that the strange love and ambivalence of *Male and Female* reflects this embracing of the Romans and the Sabines, which we are told had such "salutary consequences." The *Mural* (plates 10, 11) must be the bacchanalian festival attending this resolution, imbued as it is with the abstract ardor of the images in the other paintings of this group.

All this may be pushing interpretation to a rather fancy point, but if it is wrong it at least brings one to look closer at the works, either to prove or disprove it. Nor are we finished with mythology quite yet. It is amazing how thoroughly Pollock investigated the derivations of Surrealism which were especially pertinent to his temperament without deviation into facility or mystification. The greatness of *Pasiphaë* (plate 15) lies in the candor of its richness and licentiousness. Its varied palette produces an aura of vigorous decadence, like the pearly, *cerné* eyelids of Catherine the Great, vigorous to the point of ennui. It is not just a glamorous painting, it is glamor in painting. Far from the sterile liberalism of a Gide, Pollock encompasses the amorous nature of bestiality (which most of the Surrealists were ambitious to do, but were either precocious or queasy about accepting) and gives it credit for originality of impulse and action. In this painting, mythological still, we move away from the area of allegory into the human disaster of desire—fatal, imaginative, willful. It is the ritual of an original human act, and therefore noble—where the mythology comes in, is that the artist sees it in all its legendary splendor, not as a tale told by a tart in a Melbourne bar (as T.S. Eliot or Francis Bacon might do). The stark, staring and foreboding figure of Pasiphaë is present, with her foreknowledge of the Minotaur and her lust, as are the other figures of her fancy or necessity; a rectangle at left containing the signature of the artist is like a calendar of her doom. This is a recognition of the ritual which he is renewing. For in Pollock it is not a god in the form of a bull who seduces Pasiphaë. It is the bull.

If *There Were Seven in Eight* (plate 21), a remarkable work of 1945, is based as I believe on the *Seven Against Thebes,* it also bears a strong relationship to the *Mural* of 1953. The iconography is less discernible than in *Pasiphaë* (plate 15), which is almost its companion painting, yet it is still strongly involved in the ritualistic discovery of a recognizable event. Glowing and subdued, its double-figures are dominated by an equally double single-figure, that of Eteocles-Polynices, the brothers who agreed to share on alternate years the kingdom of their dead father, Oedipus. When they disagreed, Eteocles being unwilling to give up the throne in his turn to Polynices, they marshaled seven generals against each other. The battle at a stalemate, the "eighth" of each side agreed to decide the issue in personal combat, and the two brothers slew each other. If the cool ardor and concern with linear power of this painting is related to this myth, the myth is also germane to an understanding of its complicated juxtapositions, and its mysterious unity of forms.

Added

Thanks to the special interpretation his temperament put upon Surrealism, Pollock, alone in our time, was able to express mythical meanings with the conviction and completion of the past. Whatever qualities he saw in these myths, they were not the stereotyped, useful-to-the-present ones, which have made so many playwrights into dons, so many painters into academicians.

Gothic, 1944 (plate 17)

Here is the efflux of the soul,
The efflux of the soul comes from within through embower'd gates, ever provoking questions,
These yearnings why are they? these thoughts in the darkness why are they?

—WHITMAN

Totemism

The use of totemic figures in varying degrees of abstractness occurs in several periods of Pollock's work. They are the household gods, so to speak, of his interest in American Indian art and they seem always to present a protective influence in the painting. We see this figure in the early *Birth* (plate 6) of 1937 in all its complicated life-renewal; in *Guardians of the Secret,* 1943, the two totemic guardians stand to right and left of the central rectangle which contains the hieroglyphic secret, while underneath crouches the Anubis-like dog with one eye open and ears alert. Or are these figures Romulus and Remus themselves, guarding their young city from its hostile neighbors with the help of the She-Wolf? All these interpretations may be pertinent, for *Guardians of the Secret* is a meeting of near-East and far-West, a painting of superb unity created from the fusion of elements of Egyptian, Roman and American Indian art. That the meaning of these totemic figures is evocative rather than denotative, is true to the nature of totemic art.

After exploring these figures with great authority and finality in the two beautiful paintings of 1944 and 1945, *Totem I* and *Totem II* (plates 19, 23), Pollock in the following year seems to move directly into the "secret." It appears that the central rectangle of *Guardians of the Secret* had become the painting-subject not only of the two prophetic works of this year, *The Blue Unconscious* (plate 22) and *The Key* (plate 26), but also of much of the non-objective work which followed and which solved the hieroglyphic secret and dissolved its signs in a lyricism of immediate impact and spiritual clarity.

Action Painting

In the state of spiritual clarity there are no secrets. The effort to achieve such a state is monumental and agonizing, and once achieved it is a harrowing state to maintain. In this state all becomes clear, and Pollock declared the meanings he had found with astonishing fluency, generosity and expansiveness. This is not a mystical state, but the accumulation of decisions along the way and the eradication of conflicting beliefs toward the total engagement of the spirit in the expression of meaning. So difficult is the attainment that, when the state has finally been reached, it seems that a maximum of decisions has already been made in the process, that the artist has reached a limitless space of air and light in which the spirit can act freely and with unpremeditated knowledge. His action is immediately art, not through will, not through esthetic posture, but through a singleness of purpose which is the result of all the rejected qualifications and found convictions forced upon him by his strange ascent.

But how much clarity can a human being bear? This state may be the ultimate goal of the artist, yet for the man it is most arduous. Only the artist who has reached this state should be indicated by Harold Rosenberg's well-known designation Action Painter, for only when he is in this state is the artist's "action" significant purely and simply of itself. Works of this nature are new in the history of Western civilization, and the spiritual state of their creation is as different from that of previous artists as is the look of the paintings different from that of previous paintings. Action Painting did not emerge miraculously from the void, and it is interesting and even comforting to make not-too-far-fetched analogies with the works of predecessors because art is, after all, the visual treasury of man's world, as well as of individual men. Nevertheless this new painting does have qualities of passion and lyrical desperation, unmasked and uninhibited, not found in other recorded eras; it is not surprising that faced with universal destruction, as we are told, our art should at last speak with unimpeded force and unveiled honesty to a future which well may be non-existent, in a last effort of recognition which is the justification of being.

Pollock's works of this nature, which appeared from 1947 to 1950 and again in 1952–53, culminating in the heroic *Blue Poles* (plates 1, 75), are painfully beautiful celebrations of what will disappear, or has disappeared already, from his world, of what may be destroyed at any moment. The urgency of his joy in the major works of this period is as great, and as pertinent to our time, as the urgency of *Guernica,* not with the latter masterpiece's obviousness.

1947 to 1950

Not that the non-objective paintings of Pollock are devoted entirely to this joy. With means continually more inventive and radical, he pushed a wide range of expressive utterances to remarkably personal lengths. Despite his intense activity, the works never became categorical or doctrinaire. Each is an individual, a single experience. *Full Fathom Five* (plate 27) is full of nostalgia, its dominant color a green that is like a reminiscence of blue, with linear trailings of black, flowery-white and aluminum, with exclamations of orange, and a number of extraneous objects imbedded in the surface, like souvenirs of accident: a cigarette, half its paper torn off to expose the tobacco, two keys, nails, a cluster of tacks, and paint-tube tops making little blind eyes here and there. Earlier the "eyes" were painted to a more Expressionistic effect in *Eyes in the Heat* (plate 24), and they also are hinted at in the heavy impasto of *Shimmering Substance* (plate 25). *Cathedral* (plate 28) is brilliant, clear, incisive, public—its brightness and its linear speed protect and signify, like the facade of a religious edifice, or, in another context, the mirror in the belly of an African fetish, the mysterious importance of its interior meaning (as anticipated in *Magic Mirror,* plate 9, another "white" painting of 1941). *Eyes in the Heat II* (plate 29), on the other hand, is a maelstrom of fiery silver; it is one of those works of Pollock, like *Shimmering Substance,* 1946, and the *White Light* (plate 84), which has a blazing, acrid and dangerous glamor of a legendary kind, not unlike those volcanoes which are said to lure the native to the lip of the crater and, by the beauty of their writhings and the strength of their fumes, cause him to fall in. These smaller paintings are the *femmes fatales* of his work.

Digression on "Number 1", 1948 (plate 32)

I am ill today but I am not
too ill. I am not ill at all.
It is a perfect day, warm
for winter, cold for fall.

A fine day for seeing. I see
ceramics, during lunch hour by
Miro and I see the sea by Léger;
Light, complicated Metzingers
and a rude awakening by Brauner,
a little table by Picasso, pink.

I am tired today but I am not
too tired. I am not tired at all.
There is the Pollock, white, harm
will not fall, his perfect hand

and the many short voyages. They'll
never fence the silver range.
Stars are out and there is sea
enough beneath the glistening earth
to bear me toward the future
which is not so dark. I see.

This is the classical period of Pollock, classical in all its comprehensive, masterful and pristine use of his own passions, classical in its cool, ultimate beauty, classical in that it is "characterized especially by attention to form with the general effect of regularity, simplicity, balance, proportion, and controlled emotion," to quote the dictionary. In the sense of this definition Pollock is the Ingres, and de Kooning the Delacroix, of Action Painting. Their greatness is equal, but antithetical. Because of this, to deny one would be to deny the other.

During this period Pollock made several friezes, including the *Number 24,* 1948 (plate 35), with its drenched pools of white in black let into an ocher ground punctuated with red; *Summertime* (plate 36), a strange, serpentine flourish with colored-in areas bounded with black, as in a stained-glass window, and pointillist strokes here and there, denoting warm air; *White Cockatoo* (plate 37), a lavish iconography of color and charm, perhaps his most amiable painting—and several others, each distinctive and original in their exploration of format and possibility. In these works we see a Pollock relaxed and grand, in the opposite mood from his earlier (and later) Gothic aspiration, not building, but writing out his marvellous inspirations in a full lyric hand.

The friezes seem soft and luxurious compared to the great paintings of this period, several of them masterpieces of twentieth-century art. *Number 1,* 1948 (plate 39) has an ecstatic, irritable, demanding force, an incredible speed and nervous legibility in its

War. 1947. Ink and crayon on paper, 20½ x 26″. Collection Lee Krasner Pollock

draftsmanship; and the seemingly bloodstained hands of the painter, proceeding across the top just beyond the main area of drawing, are like a postscript to a terrible experience. *Number 5,* 1948 (plate 34) reveals the opposite kind of mastery, a structure of vigor and fullness, which seems to present the respite of accomplishment. In *Number 1,* 1949 (plate 32), one of the most perfect works of his life or anyone else's, viewer or artist, Pollock gives us a world of draftsmanship, color and tactile profundity which relates him to Watteau and Velasquez. It is a work of purity, modesty and completion. At one time it was thought that the "all-over" paintings of Pollock represented an infinitely extensible field of force which could continue out into all four areas of space surrounding its boundaries. This is true of sight, but his work is not about sight.

It is about what we see, about what we *can* see. In the works of this period we are not concerned with possibility, but actuality. *Number 1* could not but *have* exactly what it *has*. It is perfection.

There has never been enough said about Pollock's draftsmanship, that amazing ability to quicken a line by thinning it, to slow it by flooding, to elaborate that simplest of elements, the line—to change, to reinvigorate, to extend, to build up an embarrassment of riches in the mass by drawing alone. And each change in the individual line is what every draftsman has always dreamed of: color. The quick, instinctive rightness of line in a work like the Drawing of 1950 (plate 52) is present in profusion in the major works of this period, whether it takes on the cool Baroque quality of *Number 2,* 1949 (plate 45) or fuses in a passionate exhalation, as in *Lavender Mist* (plate 53). That it could be heroic (*One,* 1950), ritualistic (*Autumn Rhythm,* plate 50) and dramatic (*Number 32,* 1950, plate 59) is not so much a credit to technical flexibility as to purpose. It was Pollock's vision that was infinitely extensible. *Number 28,* 1950 (plate 57) belongs in this company, and *Convergence* (plate 71). With *Number 12,* 1952 (plate 72) we are in a different area. Following the burgeoning sensitivity of *Convergence,* it is a big, brassy gigolo of a painting; for the first time the aluminum paint looks like money, and the color is that of the sunset in a technicolor Western. But its peculiar quality is its natural vulgarity: it is not beautiful, but it *is* real. And it may be arbitrary. Yet, the arbitrary was already conquered in *Out of the Web* (pate 49) which, despite its gouged-out forms, has the subtle luminosity of a pearl.

Perhaps the most remarkable work of 1950, from a technical standpoint, is the *Number 29* (plate 58). A painting-collage of oil, wire-mesh, pebbles and shells composed on glass, it is majestic and does not depend on novelty for its effect. It is unique in that it is a masterpiece seen front or back, and even more extraordinary in that it is the same masterpiece from opposite sites of viewing. What an amazing identity *Number 29* must have!—like that of a human being. More than any other work of Pollock, it points to a new and as yet imponderable esthetic. It points to a world a young experimentalist like Allan Kaprow, who has written on Pollock in another vein, is searching for, and it is the world where the recent works of Robert Rauschenberg must find their emotional comfort. Other paintings of Pollock contain time, our own era with valuable elements of other eras revalued, but *Number 29* is a work of the future; it is waiting. Its reversible textures, the brilliant clarity of the drawing, the tragedy of a linear violence which, in recognizing itself in its own mirror-self, sees elegance, the open nostalgia for brutality expressed in embracing the sharp edges and banal forms of wire and shells, the cruel acknowledgement of pebbles as elements of the dream, the drama of black mastering sensuality and color, the apparition of these forms in open space as if in air, all these qualities united in one work present the crisis of Pollock's originality and concomitant anguish full-blown. Next to *Number 29,* Marcel Duchamp's famous work with glass seems mere conjecture, a chess-game of the non-spirit. This is one of the works of Pollock which it is most necessary to ponder deeply, and it is unfortunate for the art of the future that it is not permanently (because of its fragility) installed in a public collection.

Scale, size and violence

Pollock has done paintings of enormous size, as have most of the recent abstract painters in America. In Europe thère seems to be a general belief that if a painting is 7x10′ or over, it naturally must have been painted by an American. And the size of the painterly projection *is* a significant characteristic of Action Painting or Abstract Expressionism.

As the critic Clement Greenberg pointed out almost a decade ago, the New York School was early involved in the conception of the "wall" as opposed to that of the "easel." This may have come from the participation of so many of these artists in the Federal Arts Project which, in basic accord with the aims, if not the ideology, expressed in Rivera's previously quoted remark, had undertaken a large program of murals for public buildings. The theory behind this was, I imagine, less spiritual than that of Rivera: if the taxpayer is paying for the art it should be available to the taxpayer, physically at the very least. Clement Greenberg has noted that Pollock worked as an easel painter on the Federal Arts Project, but many other painters, among them Arshile Gorky and Willem de Kooning, worked on the mural projects, and undoubtedly this experience had an effect on the pictorial ambitions of the New York School. Certainly the great 9 x 17′ paintings of Pollock done in 1950 have the effect of murals, whether installed in a private or public collection.

Scale, that mysterious and ambiguous quality in art which elsewhere is a simple designation, has a particular significance in Pollock's work, but it has nothing to do with perspectival relationships in the traditional sense or with the relationship of the size of the object painted to the size of the object in reality. It has to do, rather, with the emotional effect of the painting upon the spectator. His explorations of this quality lead to the strange grandeur of that modestly sized, 2½ x 2′ painting, *Shimmering Substance,* whose dispersed strokes of impasto create a majestic, passionate celebration of matter, purely by their relation to the plane and format of the picture's surface. Another use of scale is seen in *Easter and the Totem* (plate 82), whose seven feet of thinly-painted, large-scale arabesques have the intimacy and lyricism of a watercolor. When we approach the all-over, "drip" paintings of 1948–50, however, a different aspect of scale is apparent.

It is, of course, Pollock's passion as an artist that kept his works from ever being decorative, but this passion was expressed through scale as one of his important means. In the past, an artist by means of scale could create a vast panorama on a few feet of canvas or wall, relating this scale both to the visual reality of known images (the size of a man's body) and to the setting (the building it would enhance). Pollock, choosing to use no images with real visual equivalents and having no building in mind, struck upon a use of scale which was to have a revolutionary effect on contemporary painting and sculpture. The scale of the painting became that of the painter's body, not the image of a body, and the setting for the scale, which would include all referents, would be the canvas surface itself. Upon this field the physical energies of the artist operate in actual detail, in full-scale; the action of inspiration traces its marks of Apelles with no reference to exterior image or environment. It is scale, and no-scale. It is the physical reality of the artist and his activity of expressing it, united to the spiritual reality of the artist in a oneness which has no need for the mediation of metaphor or symbol. It is Action Painting.

This is a drastic innovation hitherto unanticipated, even in the mural-size works of Picasso and Matisse. No wonder, then, that when these paintings were first shown in the Betty Parsons Gallery the impression was one of inexplicable violence and savagery. They seemed about to engulf one. This violence, however, was not an intrinsic quality of the paintings, but a response to Pollocks' violation of our ingrained assumptions regarding scale. So impressively had Pollock expounded his insight into the qualities dormant in the use of scale that when seen only a few years later at the Janis Gallery or in the Museum of Modern Art the violence had been transmuted into a powerful personal lyricism. The paintings had not changed, but the world around them had.

Nor is the meaning of these paintings ambiguous. Each is a direct statement of the spiritual life of the artist. Each is its own subject and the occasion for its expression. There is no need for titles. This was, in fact, the "spiritual climate" of the New York School in those years, and most of the painters involved in it simply used numbers for identification of canvases, though many had previously used titles and would return to them again, as did Pollock.

Black and White

Pollock, Franz Kline and Willem de Kooning have completely changed the concept of color in contemporary art, not by a concerted program, but by adamant individuality of interest. To generalize hastily, but I hope not unprovocatively: de Kooning, in the late 1940's and early 1950's, loved white as all-color with black as negative; Kline had an equal passion for black and for white in the works exhibited between 1951 and 1957; Pollock, following the triumphant blacks of *Number 29* and *Number 32,* both of 1950, restricted himself almost exclusively to black on unsized canvas in the 1951-52 pictures. Giving up all that he had conquered in the previous period, Pollock reconfronted himself with the crisis of figuration and achieved remarkable things. The only color that is allowed to intrude on the black stain of these figurative works is a sepia, like dried blood (*Number 11,* 1951, plate 64, a monumental, moon-struck landscape) and the strange *maquillage* on the face to the right of *Portrait and a Dream,* dated 1953, but properly belonging to this group.

The wonderful draftsmanship of the early drawings and the "drip" periods is here brought to bear on heads and figures of nightmarish variety and semblance. *Echo* (plate 66), that effulgence of sensory indulgence, the two "heads," *Number 3* (plate 62) and *Number 26* (plate 63), the reclining figure of *Number 14* (plate 65) —who makes one wonder if she is not Cassandra waiting at night in the temple of Apollo for the gift of prophecy, as does the figure in *Sleeping Effort* (plate 74)—the savagely (as opposed to brilliantly) virtuoso handling of spatial negation in *Number 6,* 1952 (plate 69) each brings an aspect of the early Pollock up-to-date, half Dionysius, half Cyclops. They are disturbing, tragic works. They cry out. What this must have meant to him after the Apollonian order of *Autumn Rhythm* is unimaginable.

The last period

Much has been written about Pollock's difficulties in the last three years of his life, and more has been spoken. The works accomplished in these years, if created by anyone else, would have been astonishing. But for Pollock, who had incited in himself, and won, a revolution in three years (1947–50), it was not enough. This attitude has continued to obscure the qualities of some of these works, for in *Blue Poles* he gave us one of the great masterpieces of Western art, and in *The Deep* (plate 79) a work which contemporary esthetic conjecture had cried out for. *Blue Poles* is our *Raft of the Medusa* and our *Embarkation for Cytherea* in one. I say *our,* because it is the drama of an American conscience, lavish, bountiful and rigid. It contains everything within itself, begging no quarter: a world of sentiment implied, but denied; a map of sensual freedom, fenced; a careening licentiousness, guarded by eight totems native to its origins (*There Were Seven in Eight*). What is expressed here is not only basic to his work as a whole, but it is final.

The Deep is the coda to this triumph. It is a scornful, technical masterpiece, like the *Olympia* of Manet. And it is one of the most provocative images of our time, an abyss of glamor encroached upon by a flood of innocence. In this innocence, which ambiguously dominates the last works, Pollock painted his final homage to those whose art he loved and thought of in his need: the American Indian (*Ritual,* plate 77), Matisse (*Easter and the Totem,* plate 82) and Soutine (*Scent,* plates 85, 86). Though *Search* (plate 83), for us a difficult, for him an agonizing work, was prepared to reveal again a classical level of objectivity, a new air, a new light, the causal insight mentioned earlier was stopped by accident—that accident which had so often been his strength and his companion in the past was fatal.

As Alfonso Ossorio, his friend, fellow-painter and collector, wrote of his paintings in 1951: "We are presented with a visualization of that remorseless consolation—in the end is the beginning.

"New visions demand new techniques: Pollock's use of unexpected materials and scales is the direct result of his concepts and of the organic intensity with which he works, an intensity that involves, in its complete identification of the artist with his work, a denial of the accident."

And his work does deny accident. It is as alive today as when, in 1947, Pollock wrote:

"MY PAINTING

does not come from the easel. I hardly ever stretch my canvas before painting. I prefer to tack the unstretched canvas to the hard wall or the floor. I need the resistance of a hard surface. On the floor I am more at ease. I feel nearer, more a part of the painting, since this way I can walk around it, work from the four sides and literally be *in* the painting. This is akin to the method of the Indian sand painters of the West.

"I continue to get further away from the usual painter's tools such as easel, palette, brushes, etc. I prefer sticks, trowels, knives and dripping fluid paint or a heavy impasto with sand, broken glass and other foreign matter added.

"When I am *in* my painting, I'm not aware of what I'm doing. It is only after a sort of 'get acquainted' period that I see what I have been about. I have no fears about making changes, destroying the image, etc., because the painting has a life of its own. I try to let it come through. It is only when I lose contact with the painting that the result is a mess. Otherwise there is pure harmony, an easy give and take, and the painting comes out well."*

This is the affirmation of an artist who was totally conscious of risk, defeat and triumph. He lived the first, defied the second, and achieved the last.

* From *Possibilities 1,* 1947-8, "Problems of Contemporary Art," v. 4, New York, George Wittenborn, Inc.

1. Detail from *Blue Poles*

2. TOP: *Seascape*. 1934. Oil on canvas, 12 x 16″. Collection Lee Krasner Pollock, Courtesy Sidney Janis Gallery
3. BOTTOM: Untitled. Ca. 1936. Oil on canvas, 10¾ x 16¾″. Collection Lee Krasner Pollock, Courtesy Sidney Janis Gallery

4. TOP: *The Flame*. 1937. Oil on canvas, 20⅛ x 30⅛". Collection Lee Krasner Pollock
5. BOTTOM: Untitled. 1937. Oil on canvas, 15 x 20". Collection Lee Krasner Pollock, Courtesy Sidney Janis Gallery

6. *Birth*. 1937. Oil on canvas, 46 x 22″. Collection Lee Krasner Pollock

Male and Female. 1942. Oil on canvas, 73¼ x 49″. Collection Mrs. H. Gates Lloyd

8. Drawing. Before 1943. Watercolor, sepia and gouache on paper, 26x 20½″. Collection Lee Krasner Pollock

9. *Magic Mirror*. 1941. Oil on canvas, 46x 32″. Collection Mr. and Mrs. Thomas Sills

10. *Mural*. 1943. Oil on canvas, 7′11¾″ x 19′9½″. Collection State University of Iowa, Gift of Peggy Guggenheim

11. Detail from *Mural*

12. *White Horizontal.* 1941–47. Oil on canvas, 22 x 36″. Collection William Inge

13. *The She-Wolf*. 1943. Oil on canvas, 41⅞ x 67". The Museum of Modern Art, Purchase, 1944

14. *Guardians of the Secret.* 1943. Oil on canvas, 48⅜ x 75¼″. San Francisco Museum of Art

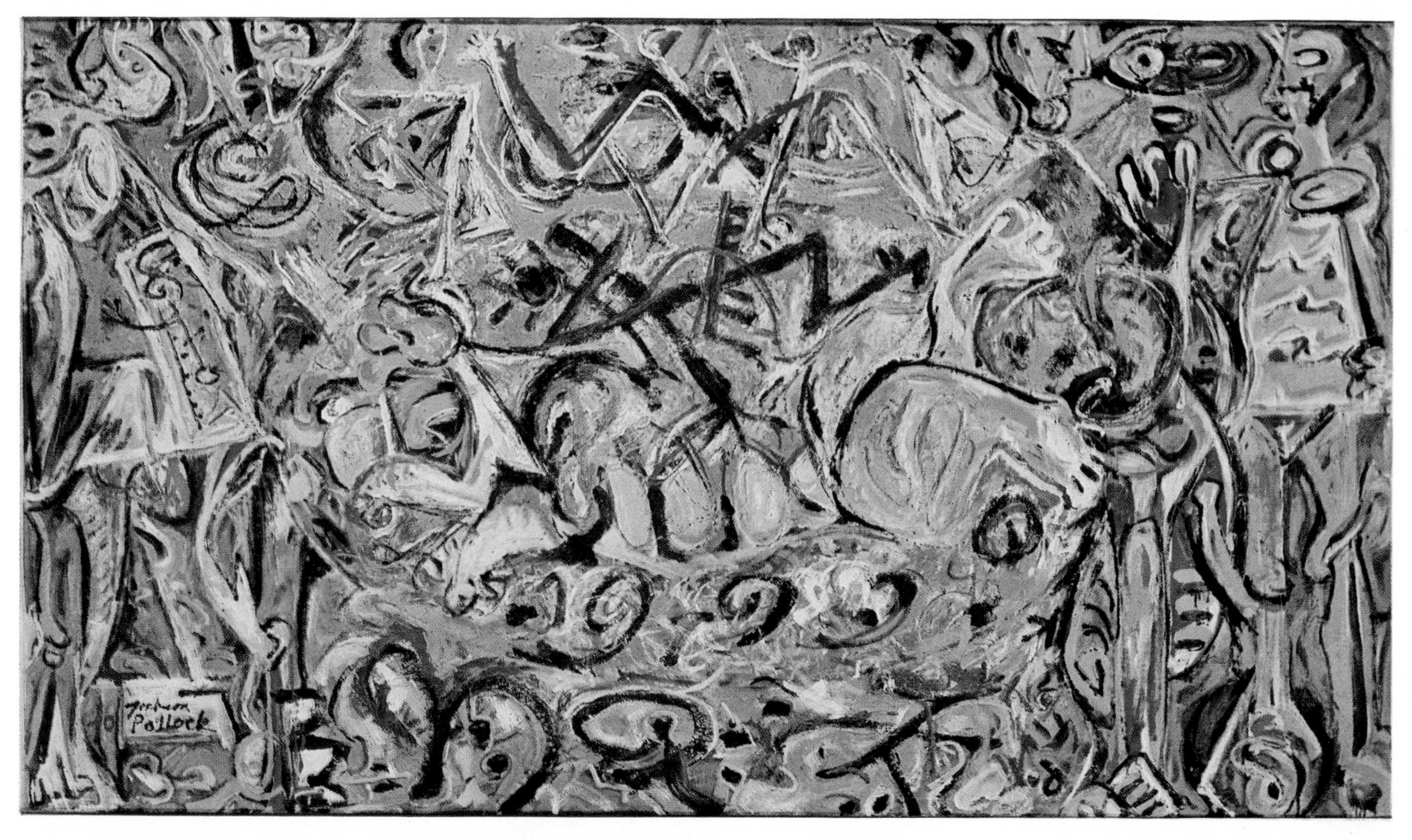

15. *Pasiphaë*. 1943. Oil on canvas, 56⅛ x 96″. Collection Lee Krasner Pollock

16. *Wounded Animal.* 1943. Oil and plaster on canvas, 38 x 30″. Collection Mr. and Mrs. Thomas Hess

17. *Gothic*. 1944. Oil on canvas, 84½ x 56⅛". Collection Lee Krasner Pollock

18. *Night Ceremony.* 1944. Oil on canvas, 72 x 43″. Collection Mr. and Mrs. Bernard J. Reis

19. *Totem I*. 1944. Oil on canvas, 70 x 44″. Private Collection

20. *Moon Woman Cuts the Circle.* 1944–45. Oil on canvas, 42 x 40″. Collection Lee Krasner Pollock, Courtesy Sidney Janis Gallery

21. *There Were Seven in Eight.* 1945. Oil on canvas, 43x 102". Collection Lee Krasner Pollock

22. *The Blue Unconscious.* 1946. Oil on canvas, 84 x 56″. Collection Mr. and Mrs. Saul Schwamm

3. *Totem II*. 1945. Oil on canvas, 72 x 60″. Collection Lee Krasner Pollock

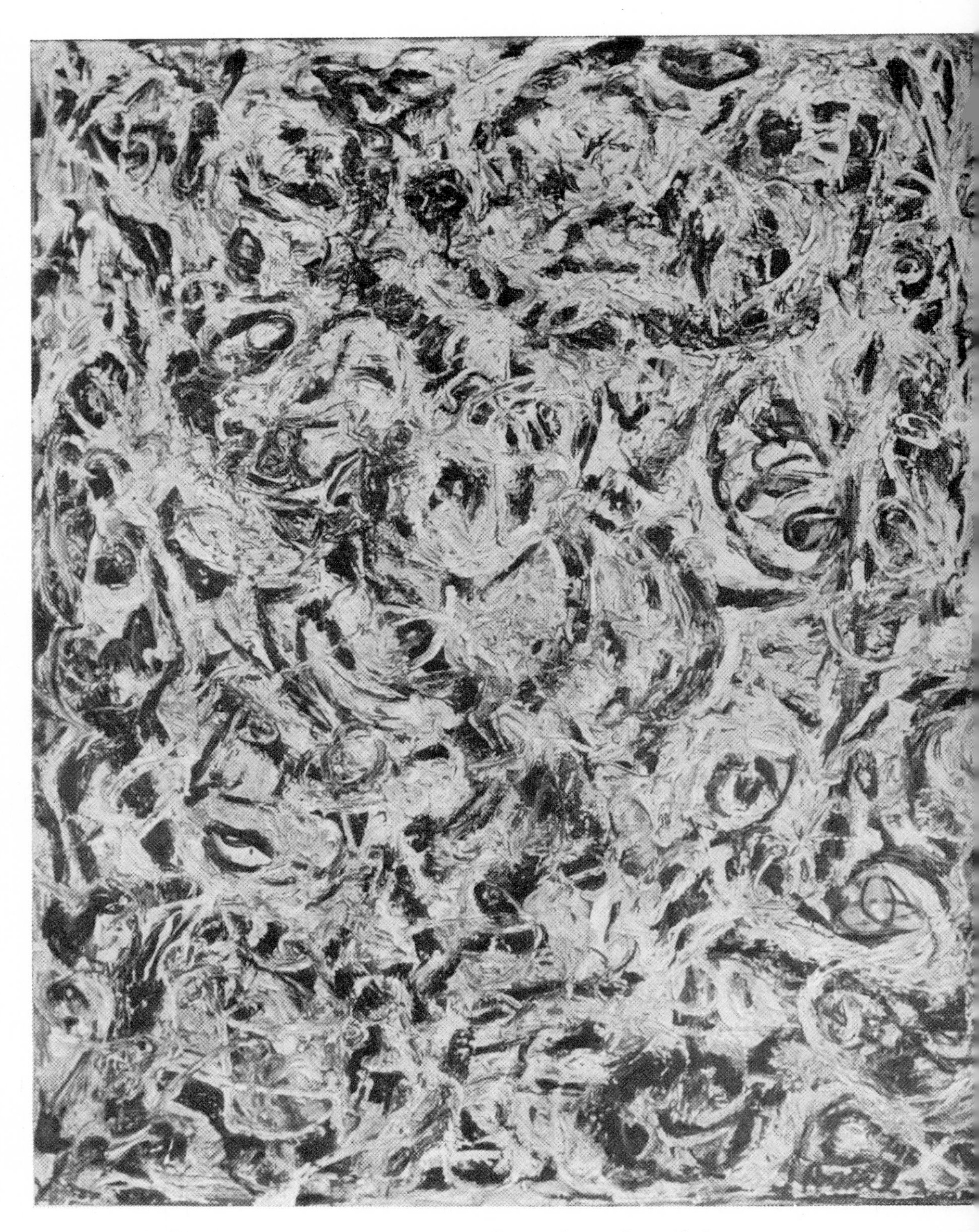

24. *Eyes in the Heat*. 1946. Oil on canvas, 54 x 44″. Collection Peggy Guggenheim

5. *Shimmering Substance*. 1946. Oil on canvas, 30⅛ x 24¼″. Private Collection

26. *The Key*. 1946. Oil on canvas, 59 x 83⅞". Collection Lee Krasner Pollock

27. *Full Fathom Five*. 1947. Oil and aluminum paint on canvas, 50⅞ x 30⅛". The Museum of Modern Art, Gift of Peggy Guggenheim

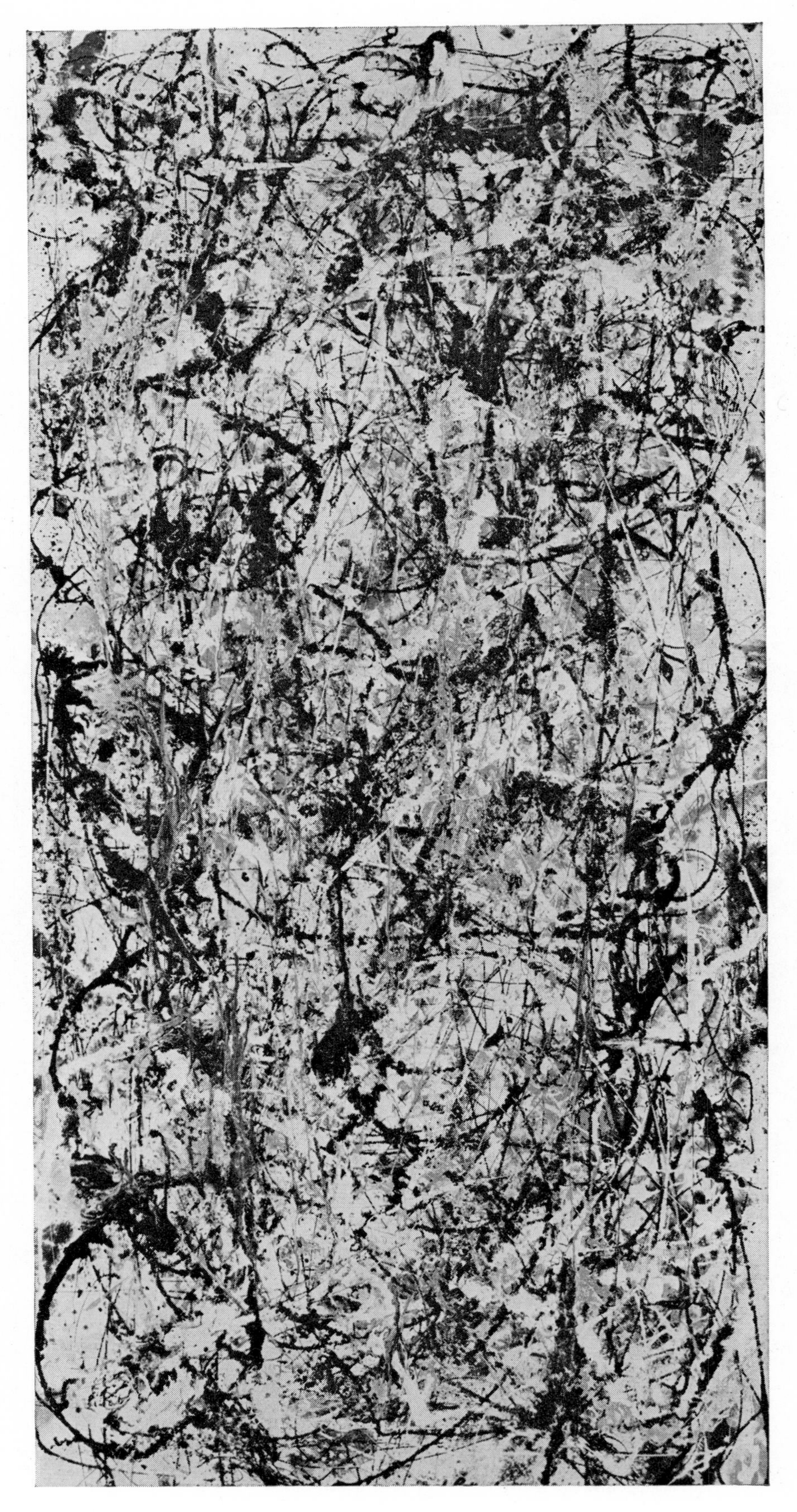

28. *Cathedral.* 1947. Duco and aluminum paint on canvas, 71 x 35″.
The Dallas Museum of Fine Arts, Gift of Mr. and Mrs. Bernard J. Reis

29. *Eyes in the Heat II*. 1947. Oil and aluminum paint on canvas, 24 x 20". Collection Dr. and Mrs. John A. Cook

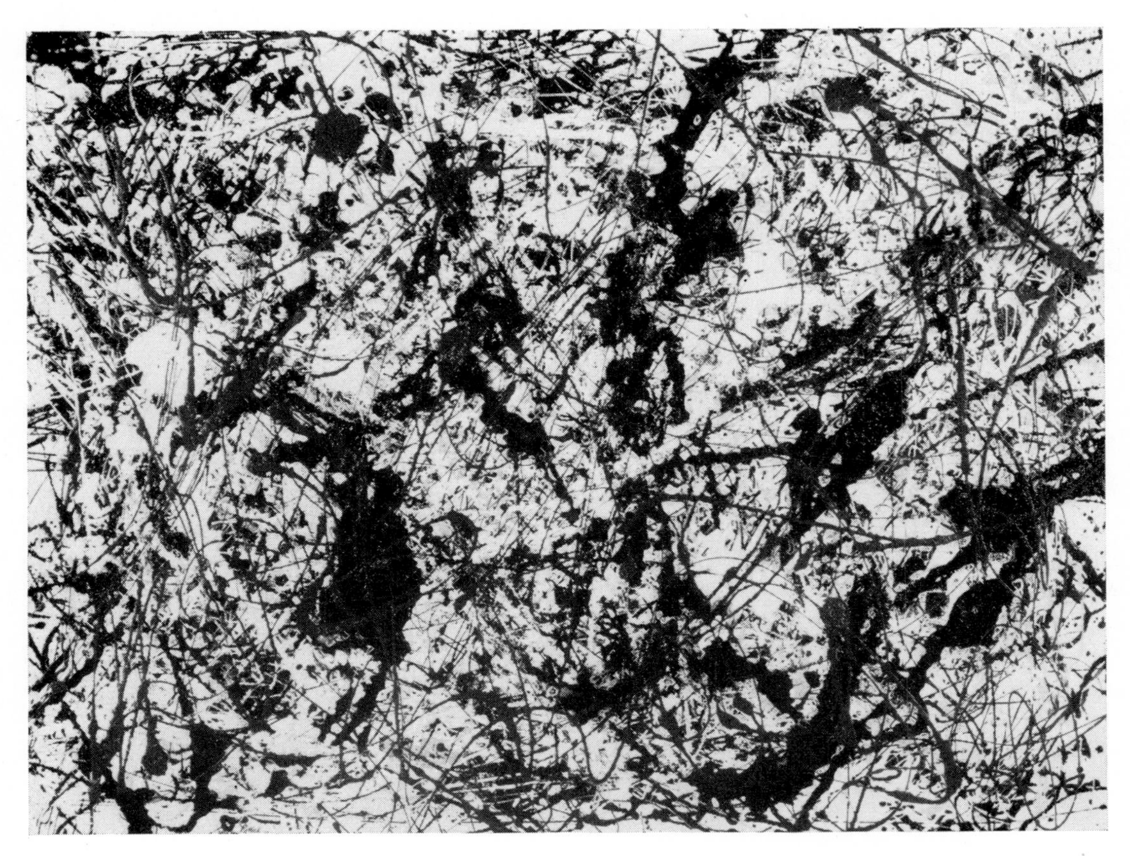

30. TOP: *Number 14.* 1948. Duco on tempera on paper, 22¼ x 30½″. Collection Miss Katherine Ordway
31. BOTTOM. Painting. 1948. Oil on paper, 22½ x 30¾″. Collection M. Paul Facchetti

32. *Number 1*. 1948. Oil on canvas, 68 x 104″. The Museum of Modern Art, Purchase, 1950

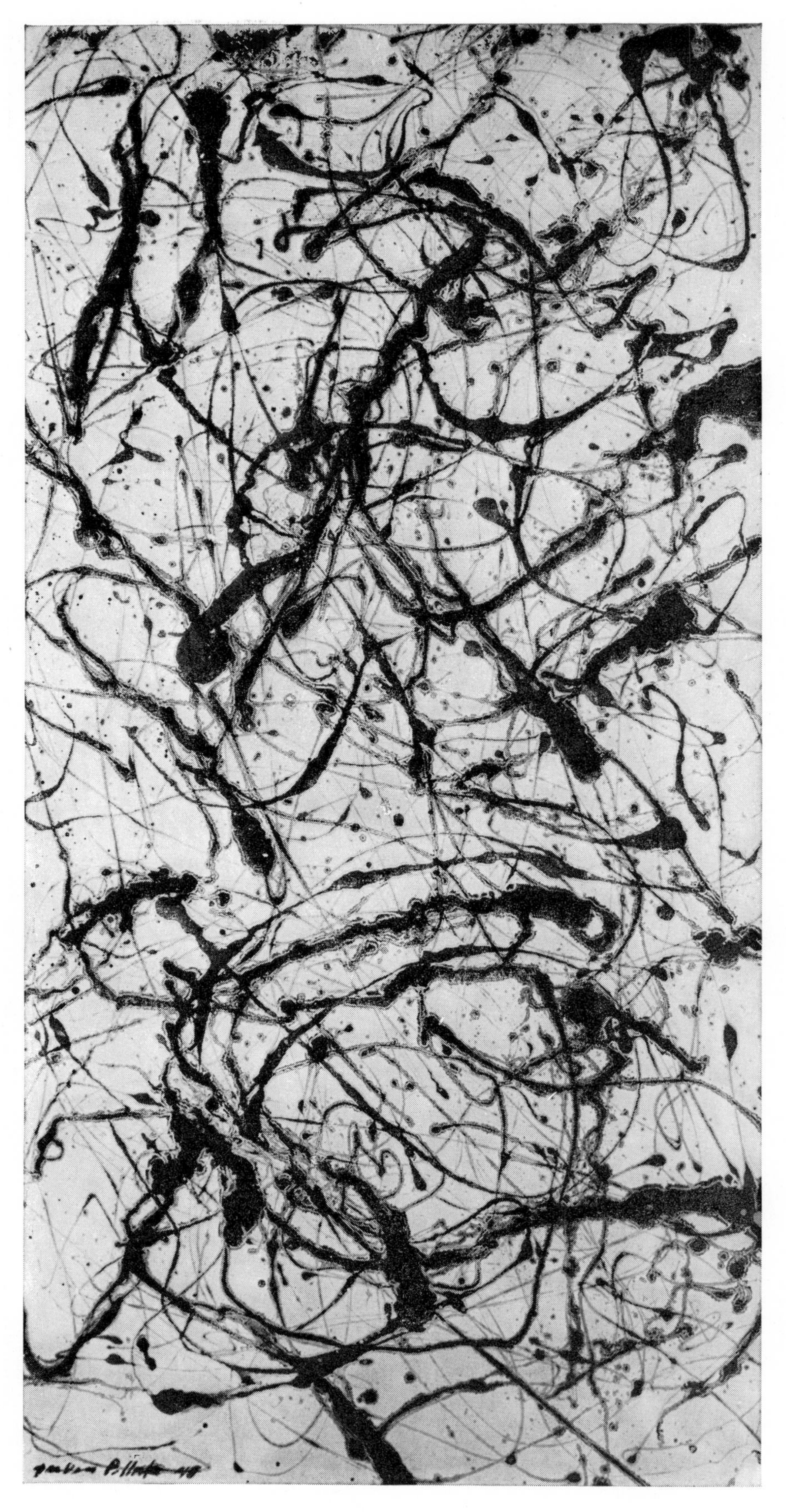

33. *Black, White and Grey*, 1948. Oil on canvas, 66 x 33″. Collection Lee Krasner Pollock, Courtesy Sidney Janis Gallery

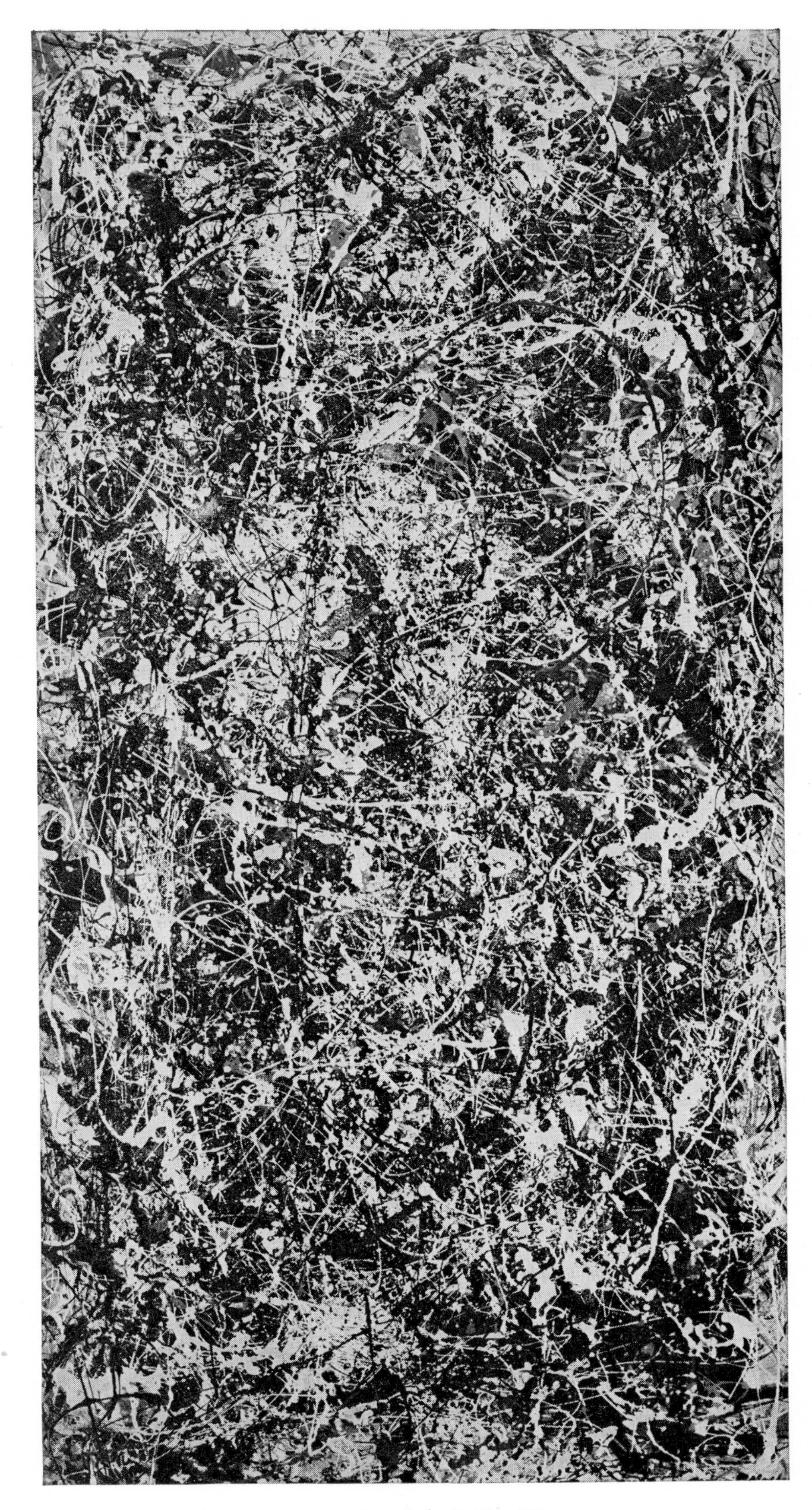

34. *Number 5.* 1948. Oil on composition board, 96 x 48″.
Collection Alfonso Ossorio

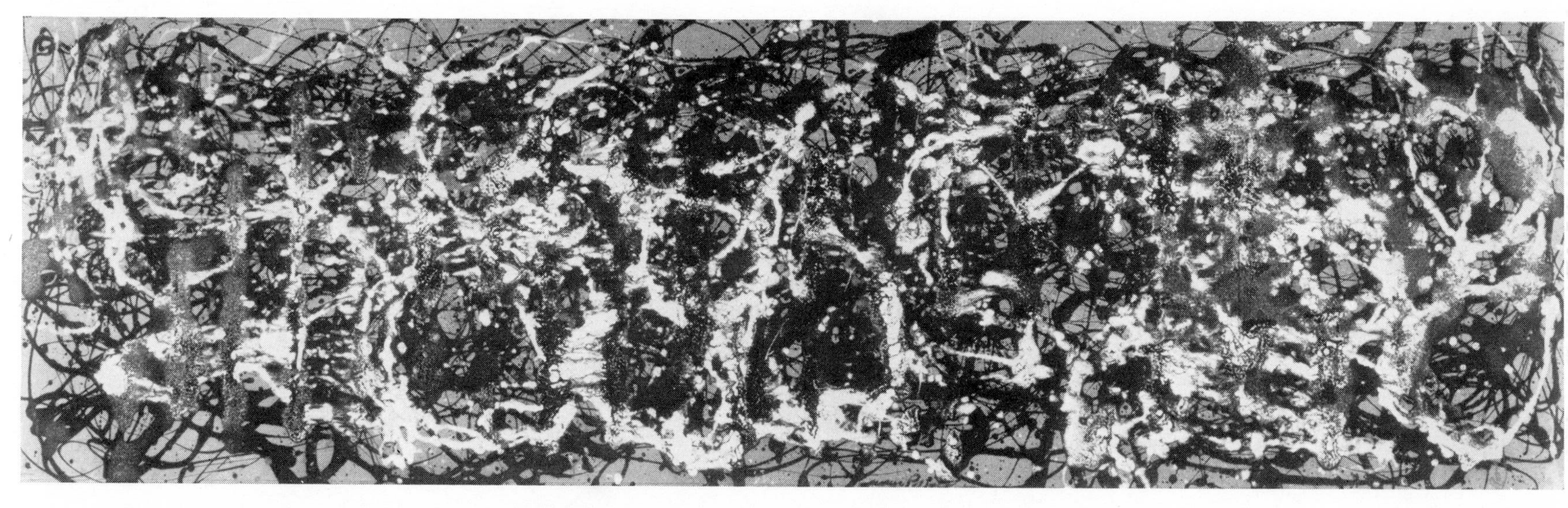

35. *Number 24*. 1948. Oil on canvas, 35 x 112⅝″. Collection Lee Krasner Pollock, Courtesy Sidney Janis Gallery

36. *Summertime.* 1948. Duco and oil on canvas, 33¼ x 218″. Collection Lee Krasner Pollock, Courtesy Sidney Janis Gallery

37. *White Cockatoo*. 1948. Duco and oil on canvas, 35 x 114″. Collection Lee Krasner Pollock

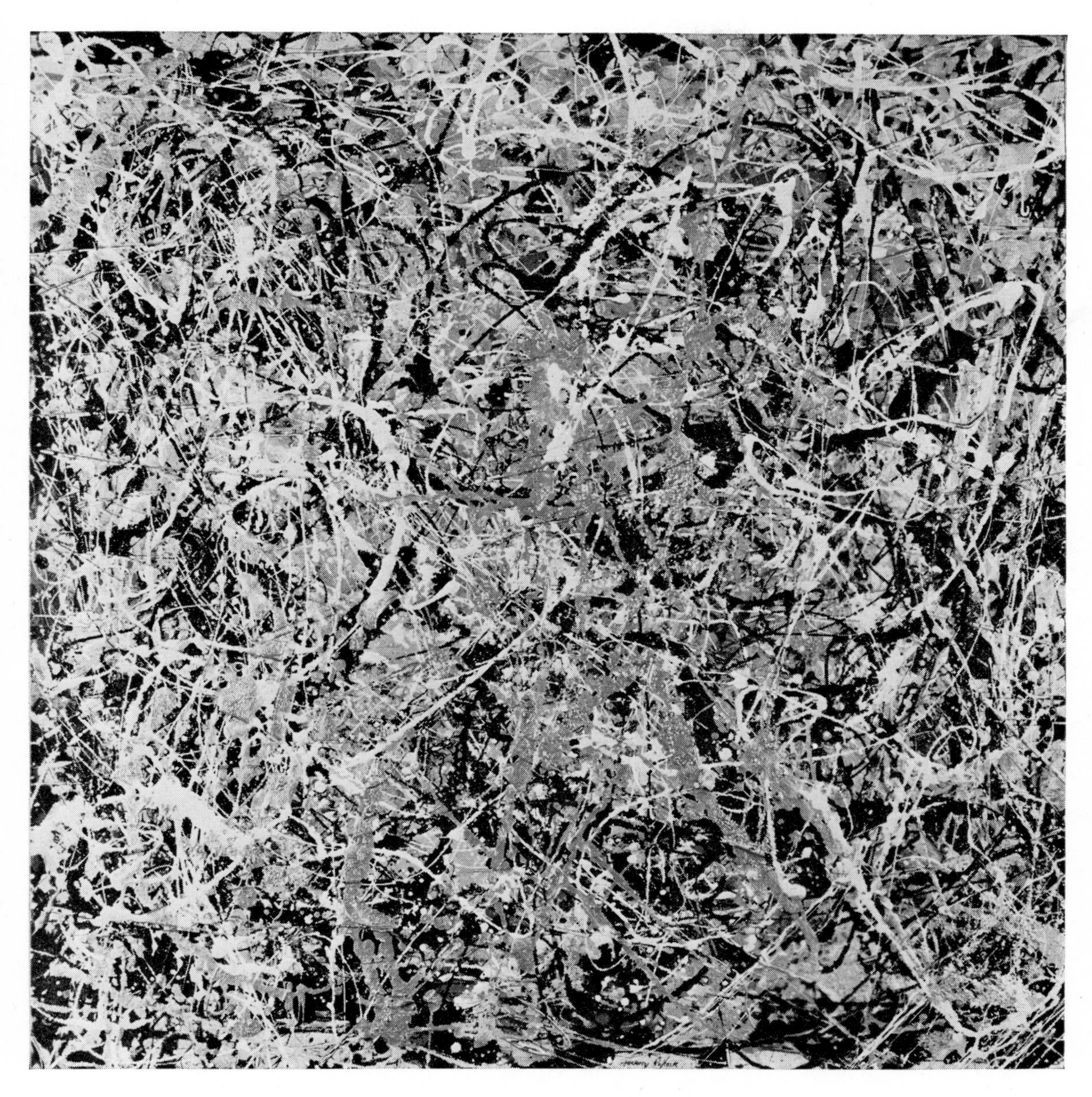

38. *Number 4*. 1949. Oil, duco, aluminum paint and pebbles on canvas, on composition board, 35¾ x 34½". Collection Miss Katherine Ordway

39. *Number 1.* 1949. Duco and aluminum paint on canvas, 63 x 102". Collection Arthur Cinader

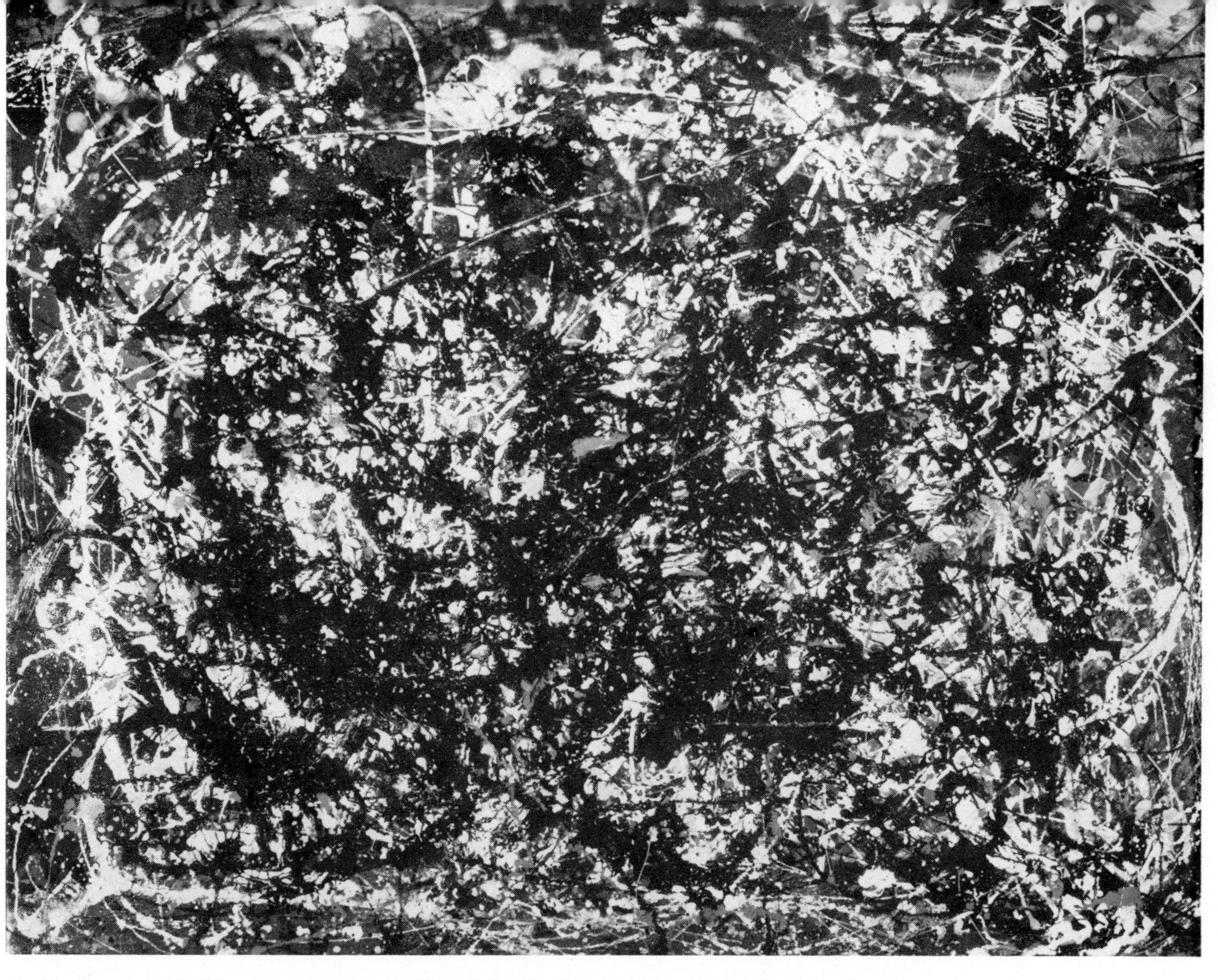

40. *Number 6*. 1949. Oil on canvas, 44¼ x 53½". Collection Mr. and Mrs. Burton G. Tremaine, Jr.

41. *Number 8*. 1949. Duco and aluminum paint on canvas, 34½ x 71″. Collection Mr. and Mrs. Roy R. Neuberger

42. *Number 10*. 1949. Oil on canvas, 18 x 107". Collection Alfonso Ossorio

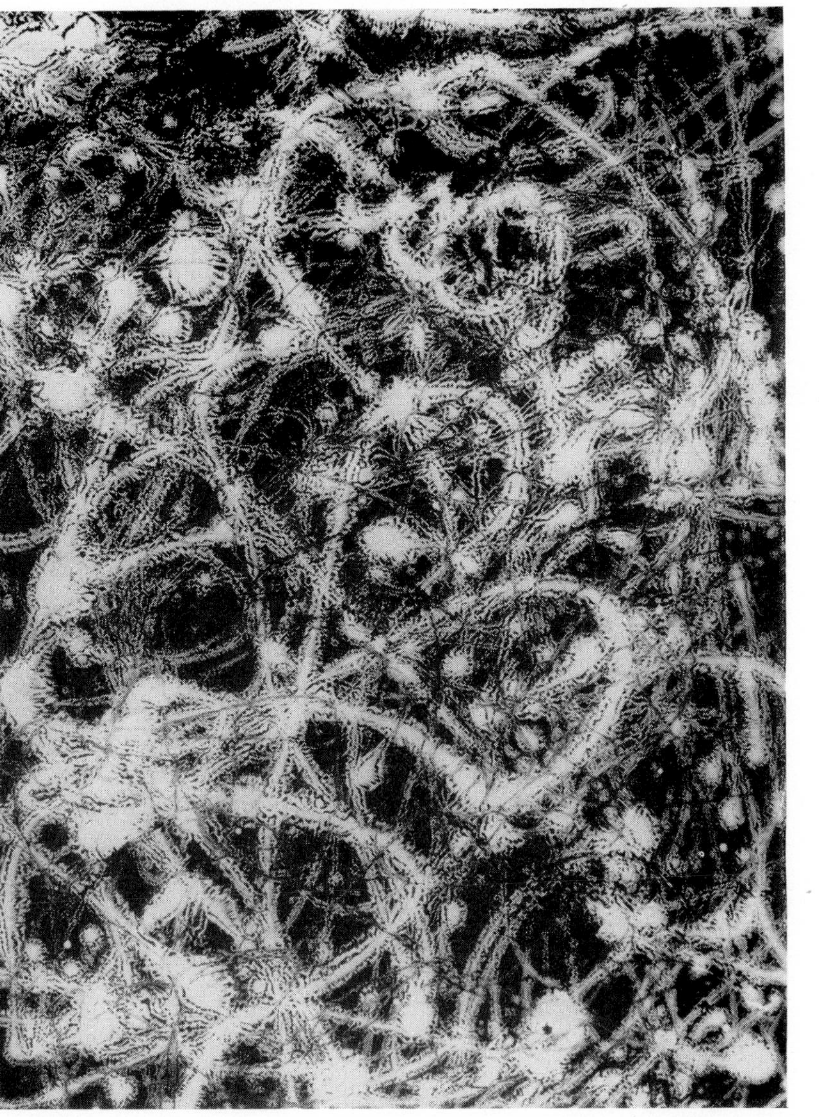

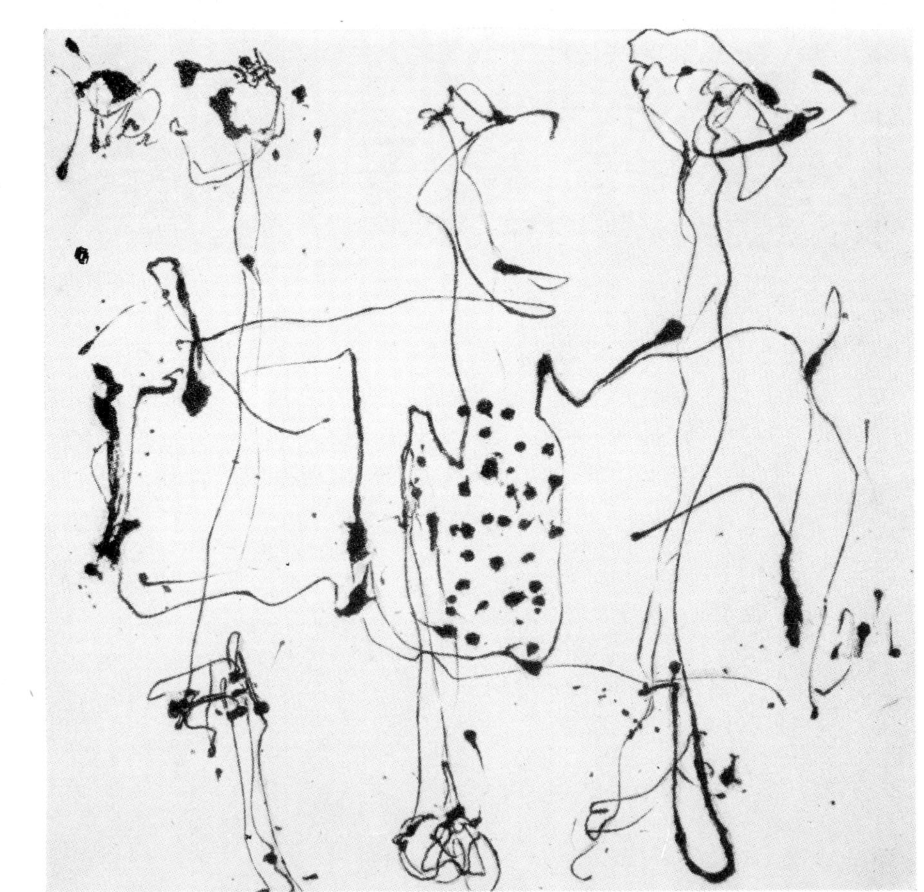

43. TOP: *White on Black I.* 1949. Oil on canvas, 24 x 17". Collection Lee Krasner Pollock, Courtesy Sidney Janis Gallery
44. BOTTOM: *Silver Square.* 1950. Oil and aluminum paint on board, 22¼ x 22¼". Collection Lee Krasner Pollock, Courtesy Sidney Janis Gallery

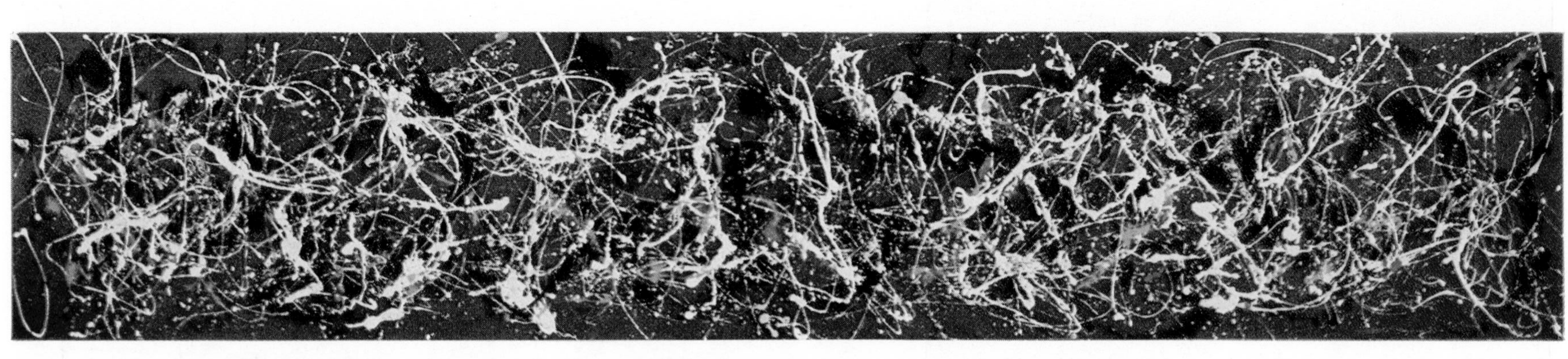

45. *Number 2*. 1949. Oil, duco and aluminum paint on canvas, 38½ x 15′9½″. Munson-Williams-Proctor Institute

46. TOP: *Green Silver*. 1949. Oil and aluminum paint on canvas. 22¾ x 31″. Collection Mr. and Mrs. M. H. Grossman
47. BOTTOM: Untitled. 1950. Oil on canvas, 21½ x 11¾″. Collection Lee Krasner Pollock, Courtesy Sidney Janis Gallery

48. *Cut Out*. 1949. Oil on canvas over composition board, 30½ x 23½". Martha Jackson Gallery

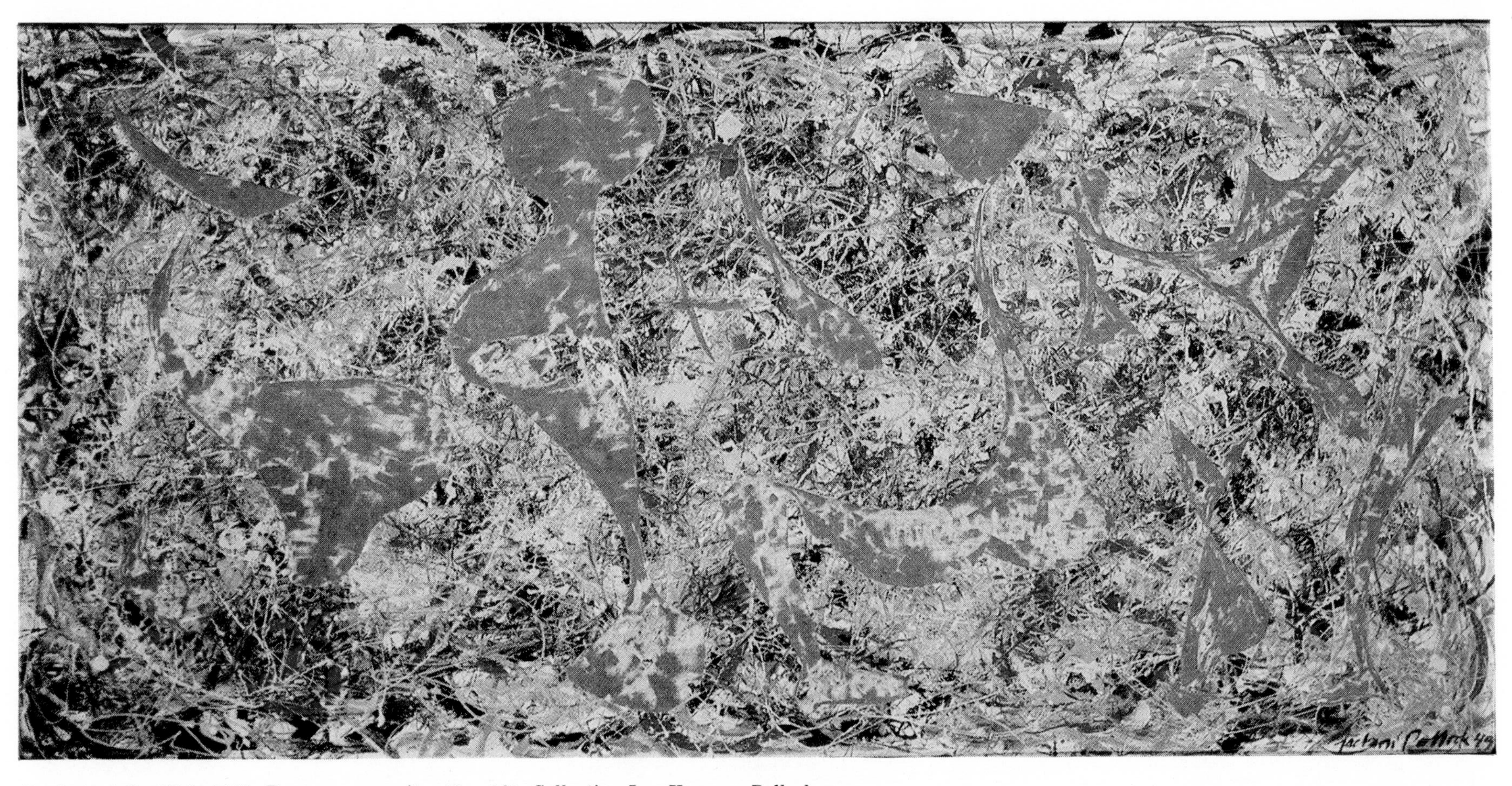

49. *Out of the Web*. 1949. Duco on masonite, 48 x 96″. Collection Lee Krasner Pollock

50. *Autumn Rhythm.* 1950. Oil on canvas, 8′7″ x 17′3″. The Metropolitan Museum of Art, George A. Hearn Fund, 1957

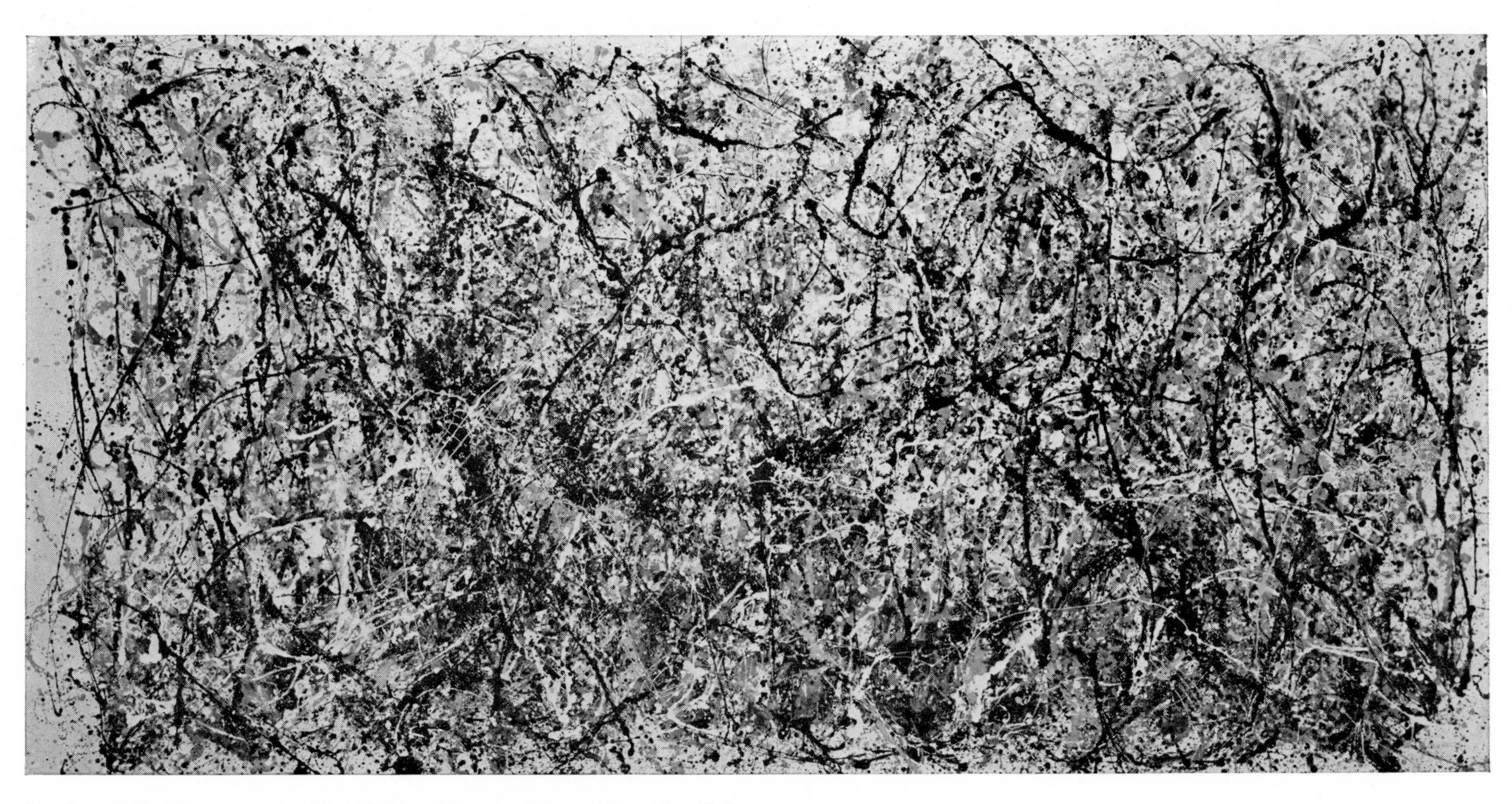

51. *One*. 1950. Oil on canvas. 106 x 209⅝". Collection Mr. and Mrs. Ben Heller

52. Drawing. 1950. Duco on paper, 22¼ x 59¾″. Collection Lee Krasner Pollock

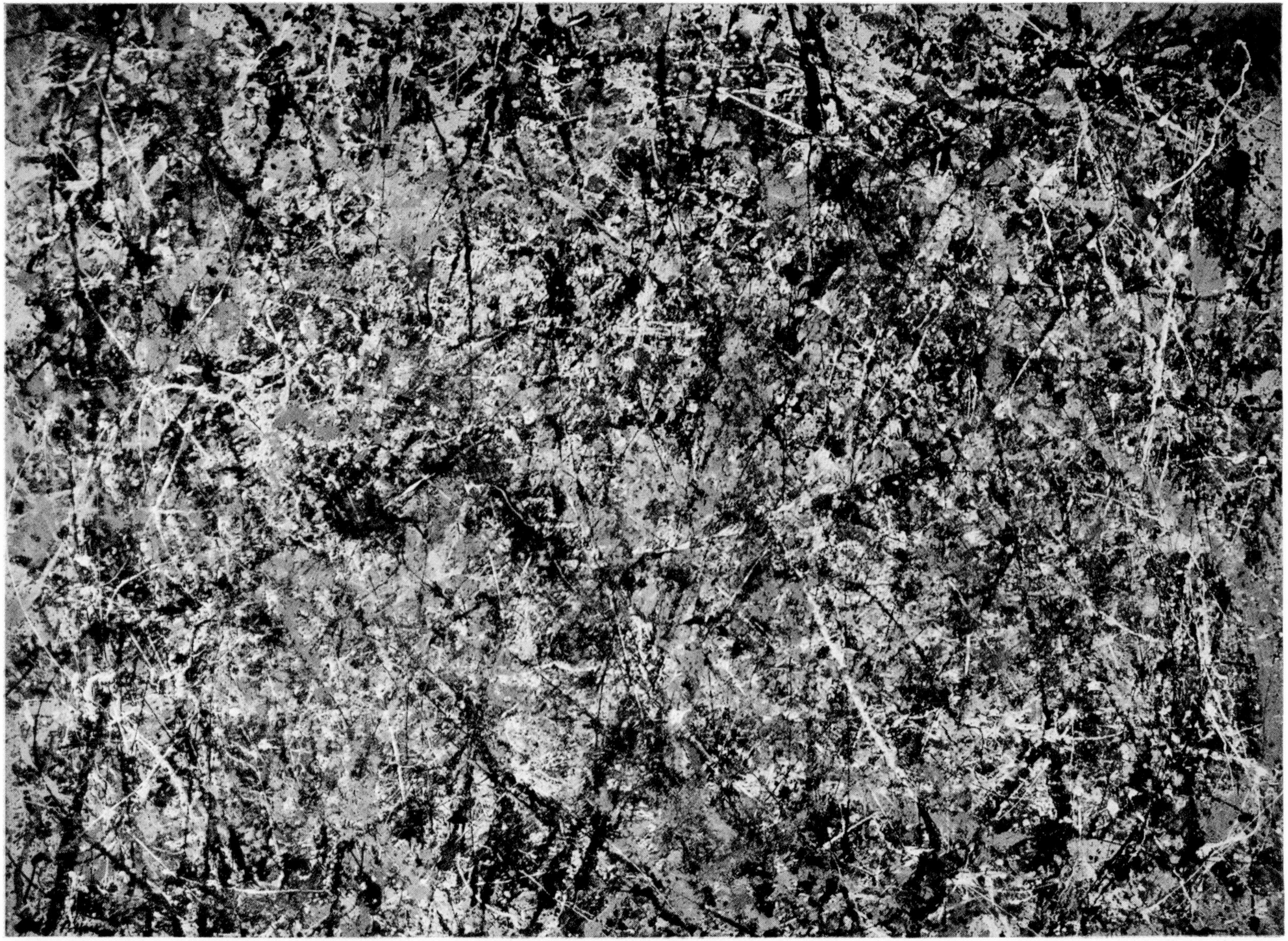

53. *Lavender Mist.* 1950. Oil on canvas, 88 x 119″. Collection Alfonso Ossorio

54. *Three*. 1950. Oil and aluminum paint on canvas. 48 x 96″. Private Collection

55. *Number 8*. 1950. Oil on canvas, 56 x 39". Collection Mr. and Mrs. Ira Haupt

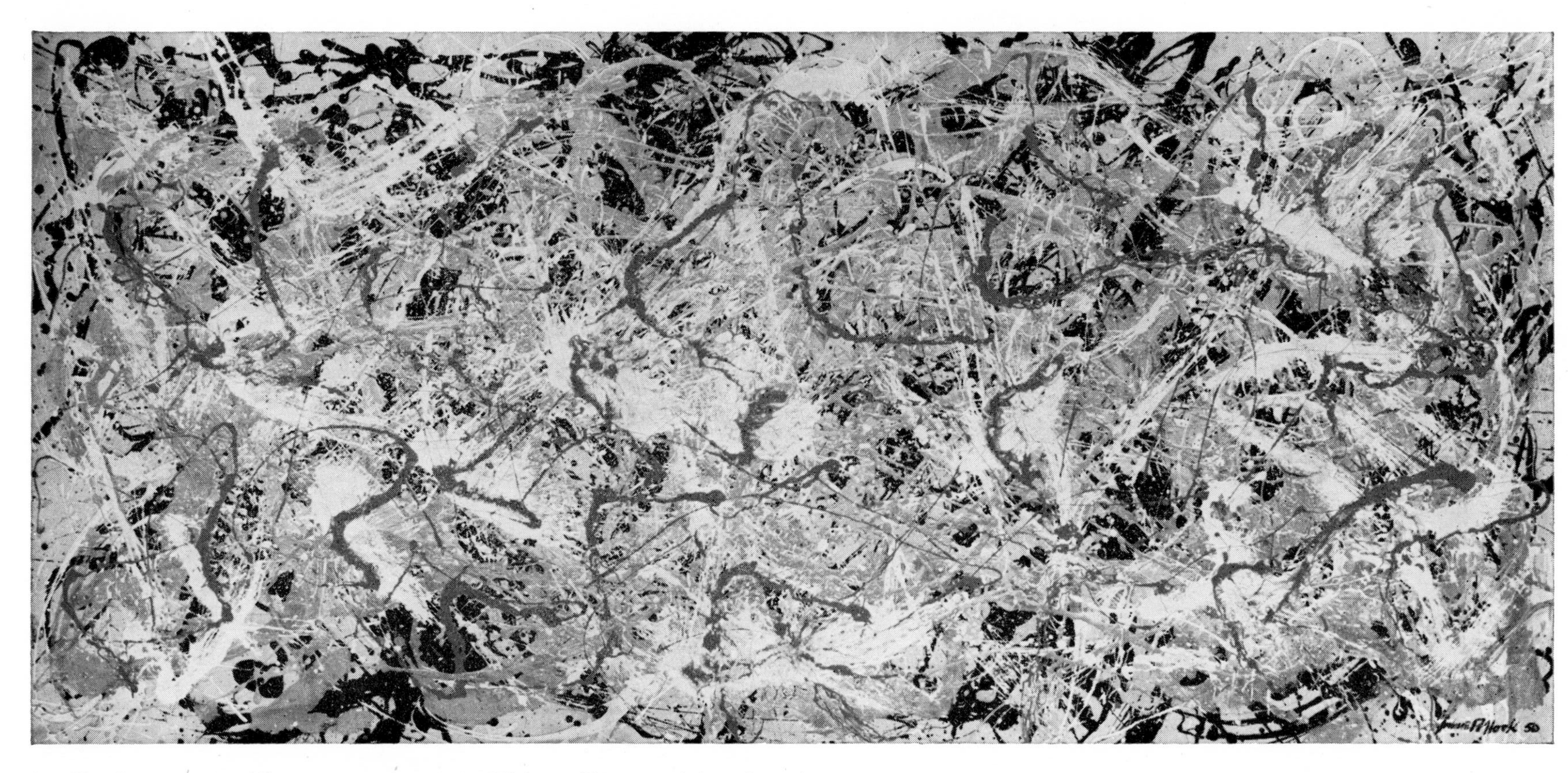

56. *Number 27.* 1950. Oil on canvas, 49 x 106″. Whitney Museum of American Art

57. *Number 28.* 1950. Oil on canvas, 68″ x 8′9″. Collection Mrs. Albert H. Newman

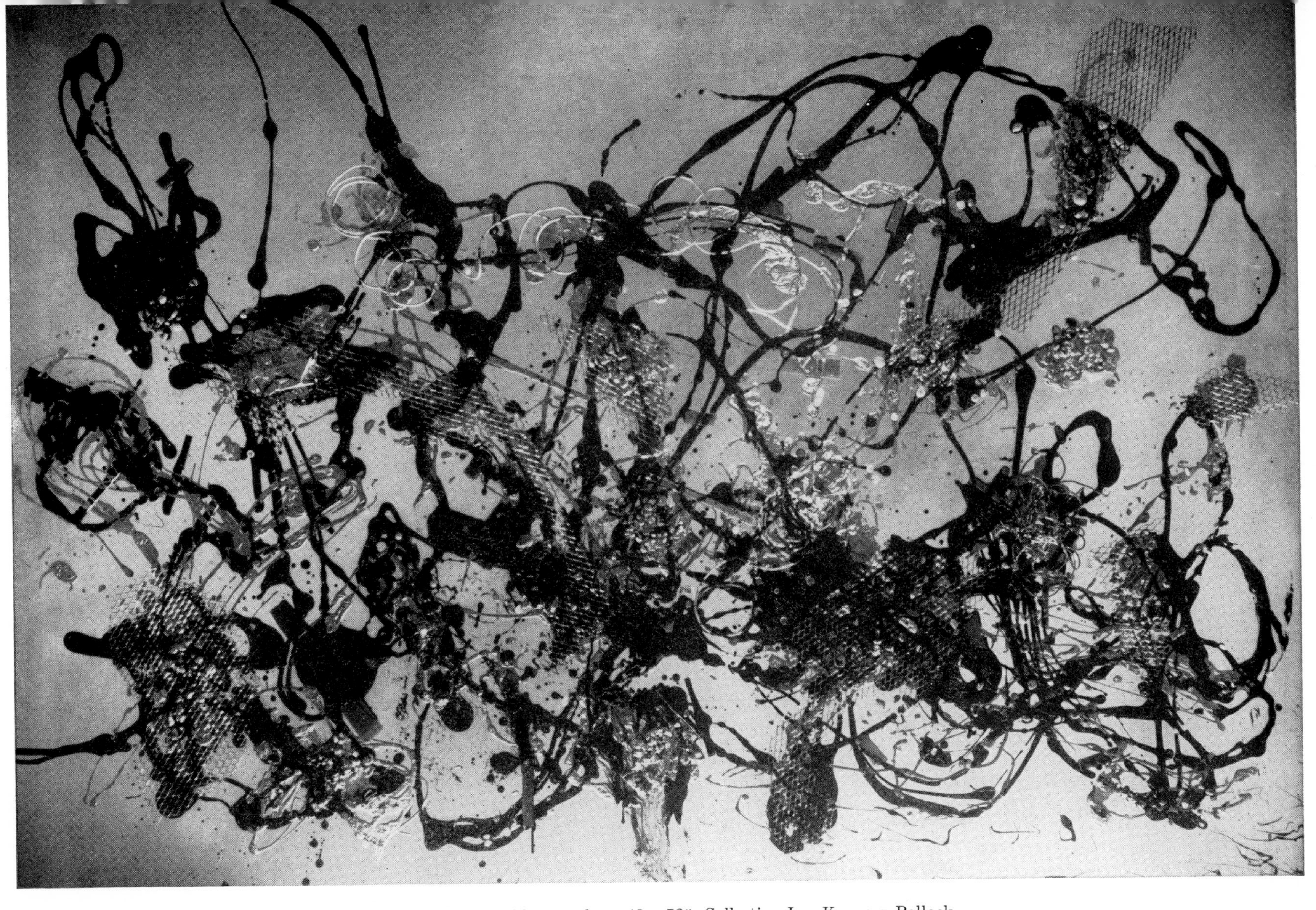

58. *Number 29*. 1950. Oil paint, wire mesh, string shells, pebbles on glass, 48 x 72". Collection Lee Krasner Pollock

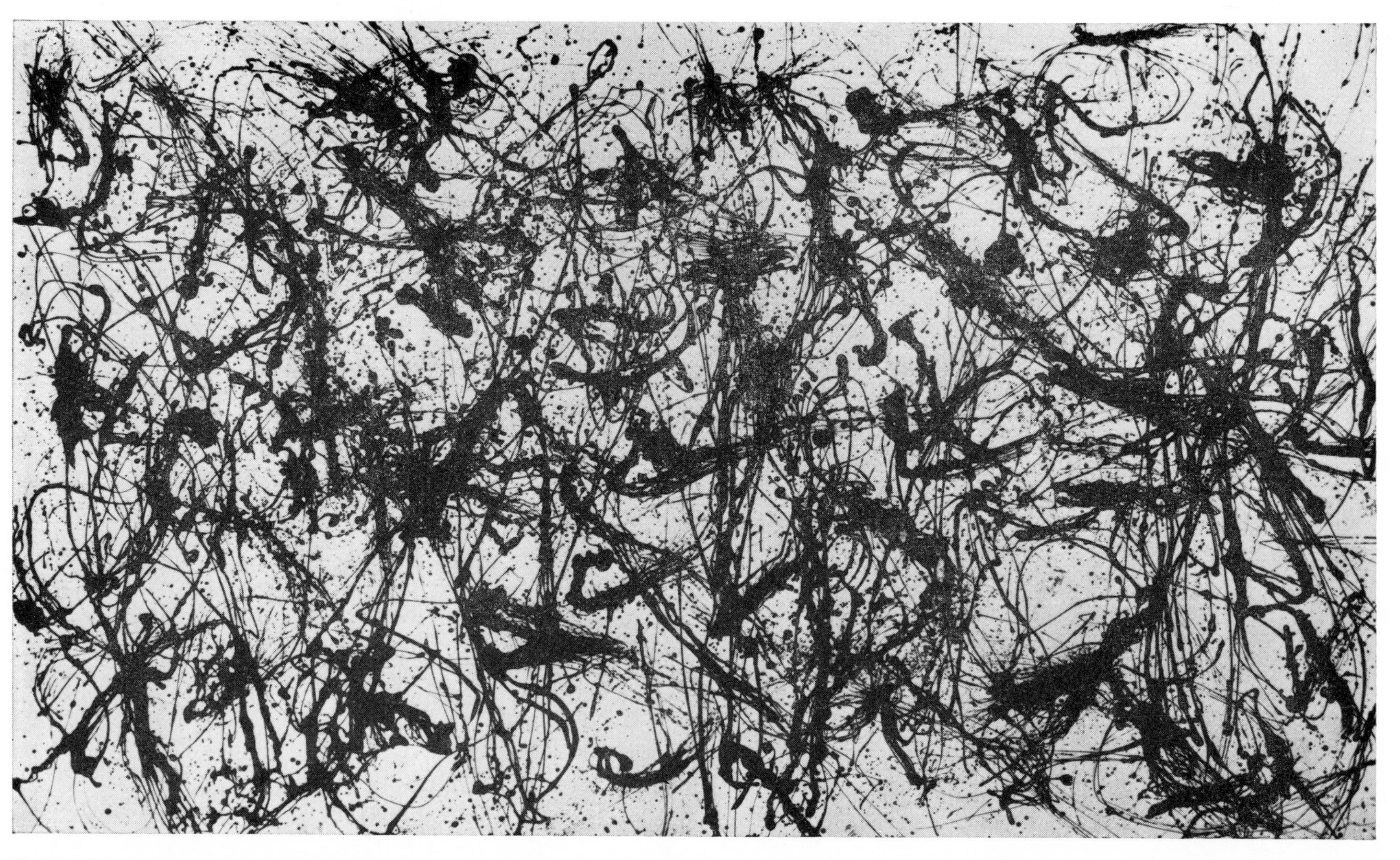

59. *Number 32*. 1950. Duco on canvas, 106 x 180″. Collection Lee Krasner Pollock

60. Detail from *Number 32*

61. *Number 32* (*"Frogman"*). 1951. Oil on canvas. 58½ x 47". Martha Jackson Gallery

62. TOP: Painting. 1951. Watercolor, 24⅝ x 39⅛". Collection Lee Krasner Pollock
63. BOTTOM: *Number 26*. 1951. Oil on canvas, 54¼ x 36½". Collection Lee Krasner Pollock, Courtesy Sidney Janis Gallery

64. *Number 11.* 1951. Duco on canvas, 57⅝ x 138⅛″. Collection Lee Krasner Pollock, Courtesy Sidney Janis Gallery

65. *Number 14*. 1951. Oil on canvas, 57⅞ x 106″. Collection Lee Krasner Pollock

66. *Echo.* 1951. Oil on canvas, 92 x 85¾". Collection Lee Krasner Pollock

67. *Number 27*. 1951. Oil on canvas, 55¾ x 75¼". Collection Lee Krasner Pollock, Courtesy Sidney Janis Gallery

68. *Black and White Painting*. 1951–52. Oil on canvas, 35 x 31″. Collection Dr. and Mrs. R. H. Patterson

69. *Number 6*. 1952. Oil on canvas, 56 x 47". Collection Mrs. Leo Castelli

70. *Ocean Greyness*. 1953. Oil and duco on canvas, 57¾ x 90⅛". The Solomon R. Guggenheim Museum

71. *Convergence.* 1952. Oil on canvas, 94 x 156″. Albright Art Gallery

72. *Number 12.* 1952. Oil on canvas, 101⅞ x 89″. Private Collection, N.Y.

73. *Black and White, Number 5.* 1952. Oil on canvas, 56 x 31½". Collection Lee Krasner Pollock, Courtesy Sidney Janis Gallery

74. *Sleeping Effort.* 1953. Oil on canvas, 50 x 76¼". Washington University Art Collection

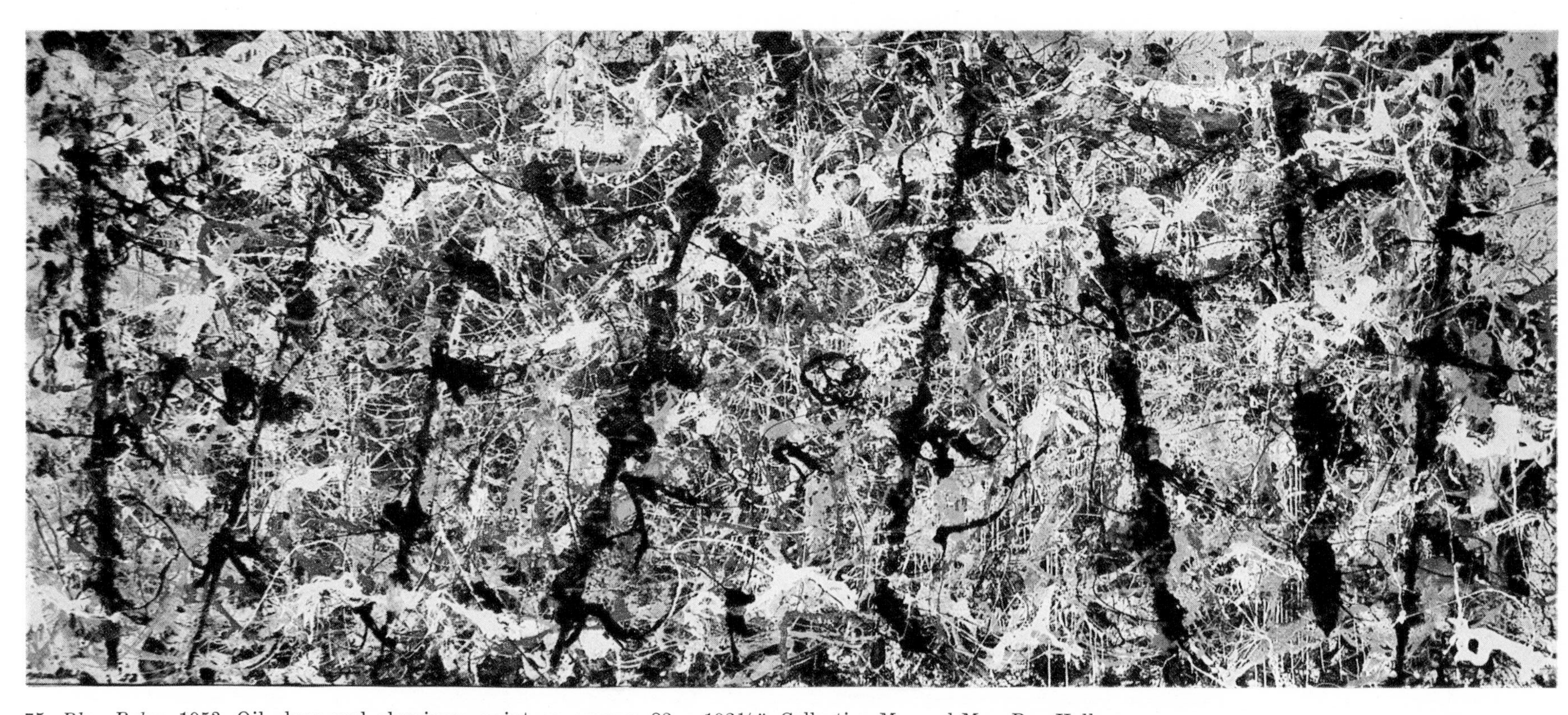

75. *Blue Poles.* 1953. Oil, duco and aluminum paint on canvas, 83 x 192½″. Collection Mr. and Mrs. Ben Heller

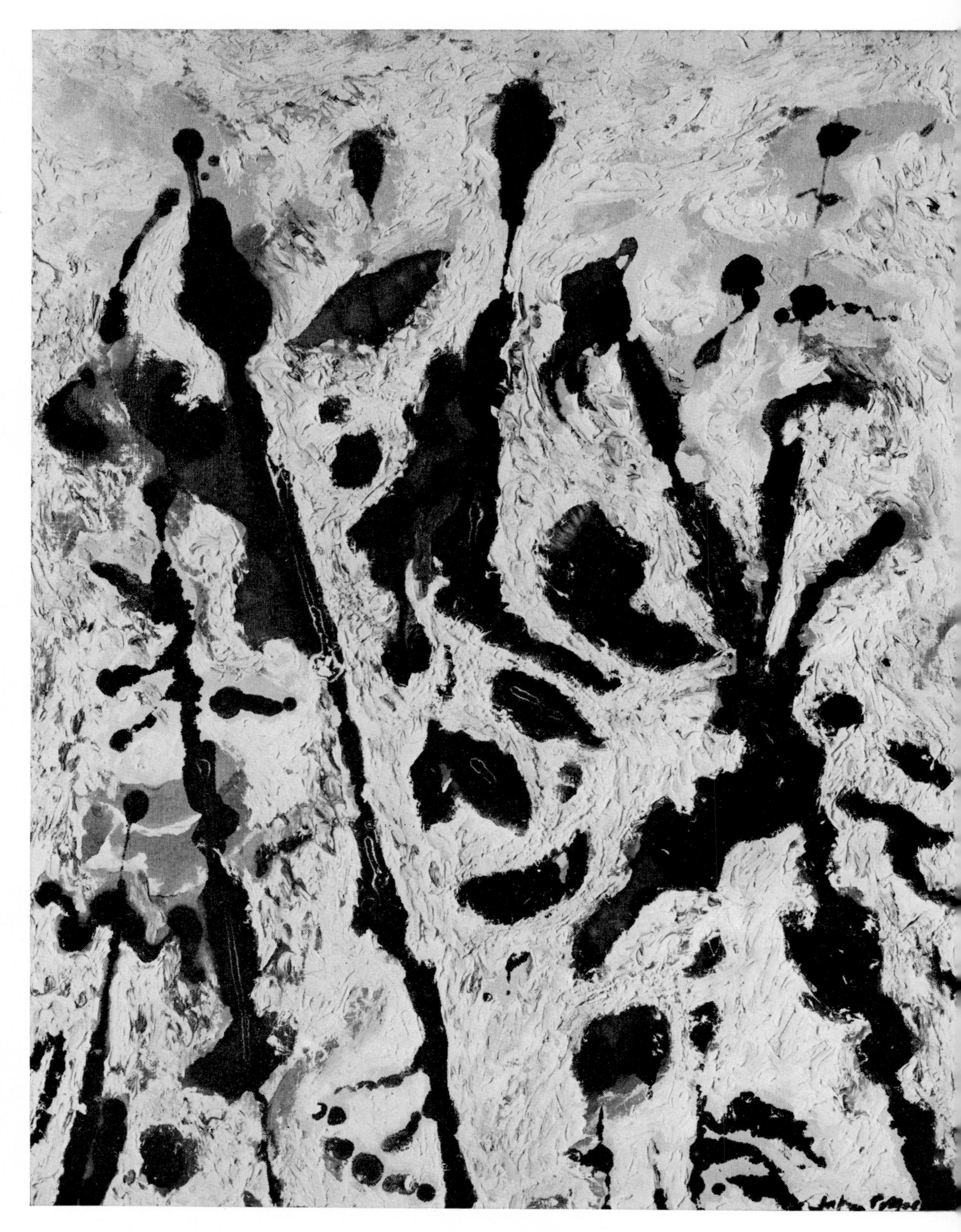

76. *Moon Vibrations.* 1953. Oil on canvas. 43 x 34″. Collection Mr. and Mrs. Charles Bagley Wright

77. *Ritual.* 1953. Oil on canvas. 90 x 42″. Collection Mr. and Mrs. Stanley J. Wolf

78. *Four Opposites.* 1953. Oil, duco and aluminum paint on canvas, 72¼ x 51¼".
Collection Mr. and Mrs. Boris Leavitt

79. *The Deep*. 1953. Duco and oil on canvas, 86¾ x 58⅛". Collection Lee Krasner Pollock, Courtesy Sidney Janis Gallery

80. *Unformed Figure.* 1953. Oil on canvas, 52 x 77". Collection E. J. Power

81. *Greyed Rainbow.* 1953. Oil on canvas, 72 x 96″. The Art Institute of Chicago, Gift of the Society for Contemporary American Art

82. *Easter and the Totem.* 1953. Oil on canvas, 82⅛ x 57⅞". Collection Lee Krasner Pollock, Courtesy Sidney Janis Gallery

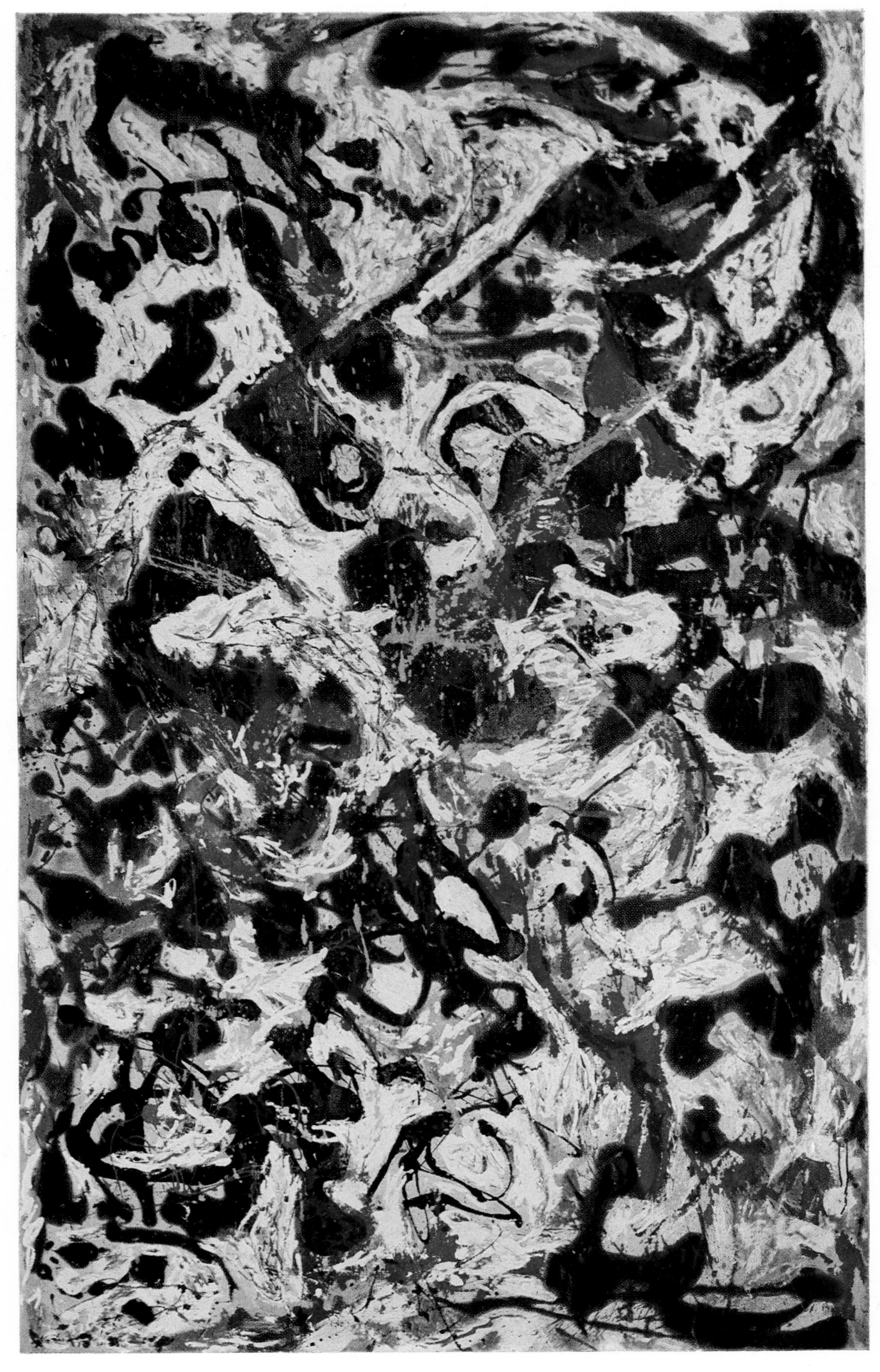

83. *Search.* 1955. Oil on canvas, 57½ x 90″. Collection Mr. and Mrs. Albert F. Sperry

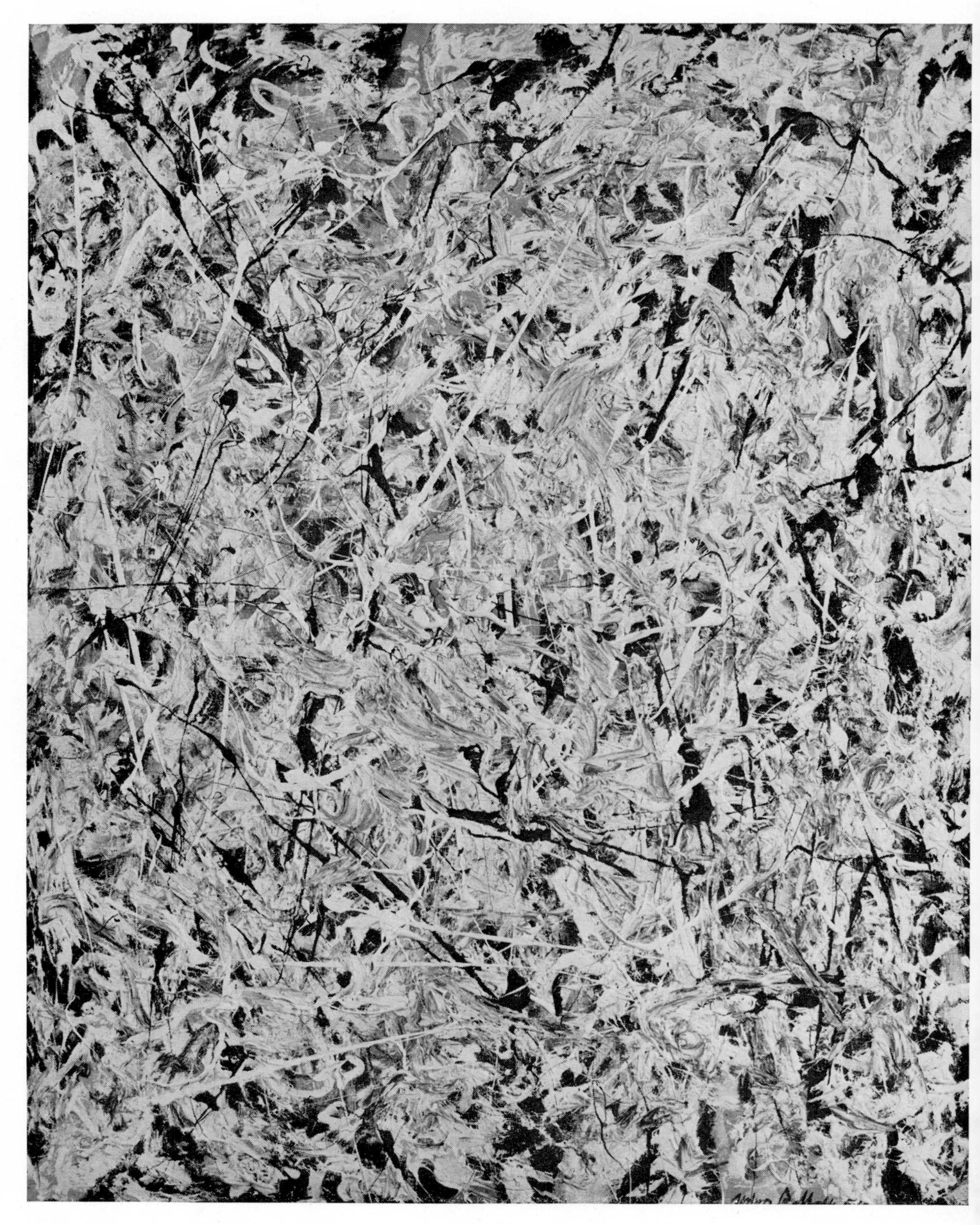

84. *White Light*. 1954. Oil on canvas, 48½ x 38″. Collection anonymous, N.Y.

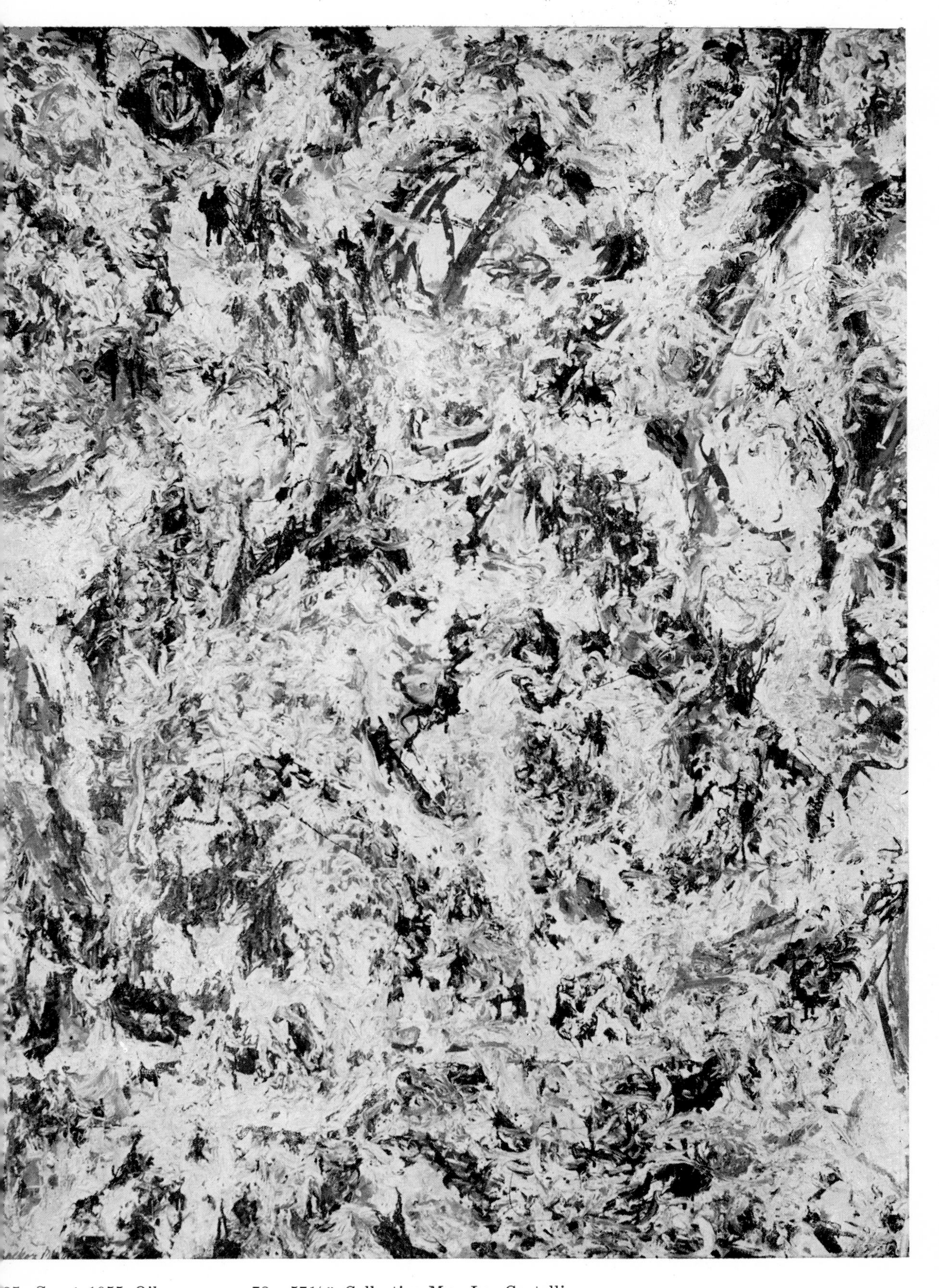

85. *Scent.* 1955. Oil on canvas, 78 x 57½". Collection Mrs. Leo Castelli

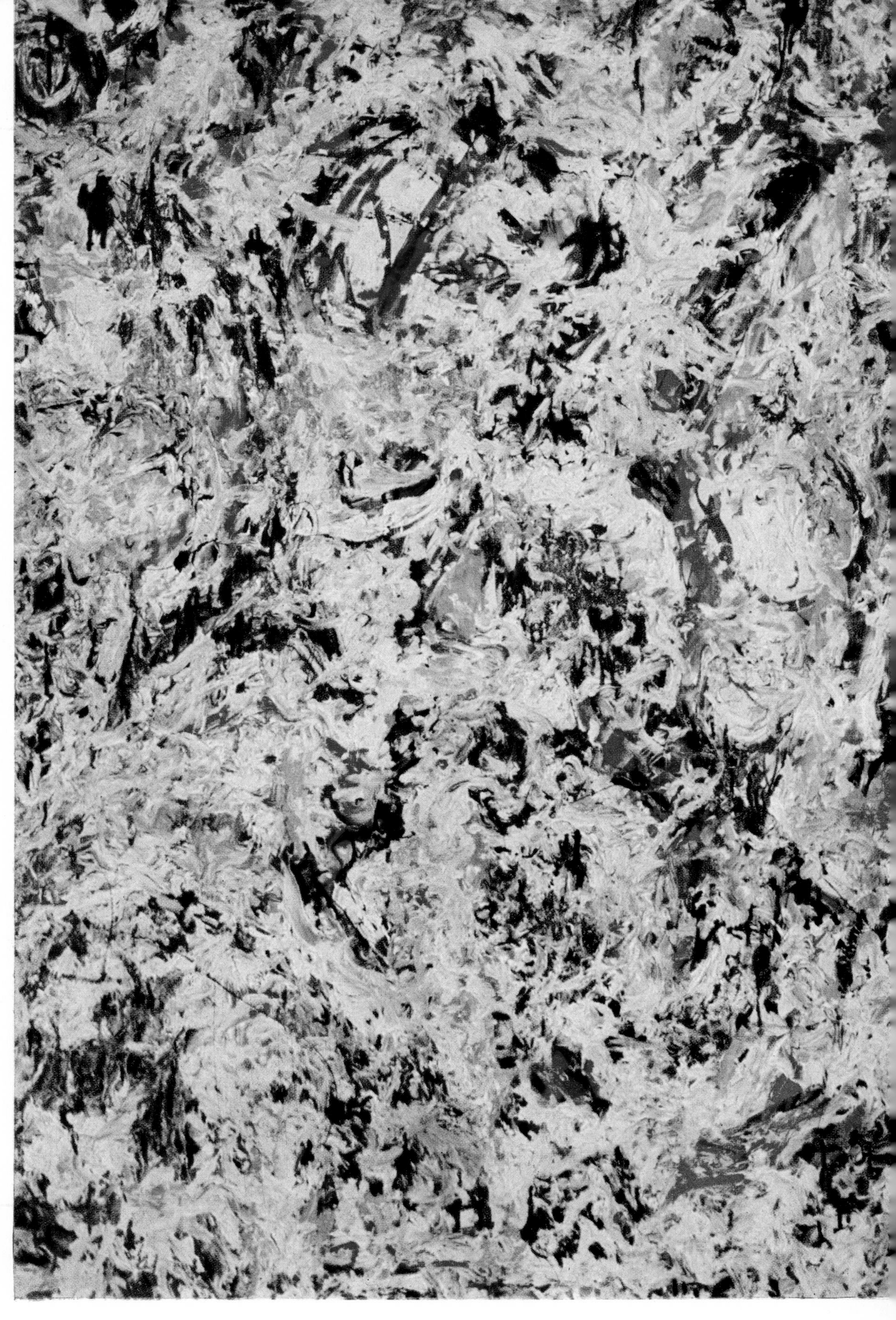

86. Detail from *Scent*

Drawing. 1952. Ink on paper, 17½ x 22⅜″. Collection Lee Krasner Pollock

CHRONOLOGY

1912 Jackson Pollock was born on January 28th in Cody, Wyoming, the fifth son of Stella (née McClure) and Le Roy Pollock. His father was born Le Roy McCoy, but was adopted by the Pollock family as a child. Originally a farmer, he became a surveyor, and Jackson spent his childhood in the West, chiefly in Arizona and Northern California. In 1925 the family settled in Southern California.

1925–29 Pollock became interested in art through his brother Charles, the oldest of the five, and attended Manual Arts High School in Los Angeles. Another painter who was later to become a leading figure in the New York School was also studying there, Philip Guston. At first Pollock's chief interest was sculpture, but it soon shifted to painting.

1929–31 He left Los Angeles without graduating from high school and came to New York, where he studied with Thomas Benton at the Art Students League. This move was chiefly at the instigation of his brother Charles, who had also worked with Benton in New York, and was the beginning of a long relationship with Benton, first as student, later as friend.

There are a few photographs of paintings done by Pollock in the next couple of years which indicate that he was somewhat influenced by Benton's regionalist style, and more so by the work of Ryder (plate 2). During these years he made several trips West, settling more or less permanently in New York in 1935.

1938–42 Pollock worked on the Federal Arts Project during these years. The excellence of this project, headed by such men as Holger Cahill, whose enthusiasm and authority in artistic matters should have been a model for governmental agencies of this kind, may be recalled by listing at random some of the painters to whom it gave employment without divorcing them from their art or interrupting their development: Arshile Gorky, Willem de Kooning, William Baziotes, Philip Guston, James Brooks, Mark Rothko, Giorgio Cavallon, Jack Tworkov, and of course many others.

Pollock showed his work for the first time in New York in 1940. This exhibition, at the McMillan Gallery, included works by French and American artists—among the latter were Willem de Kooning and Lee Krasner. Miss Krasner, who was later to become his wife, first met Pollock at this time.

The influx of European artists at the beginning of the war added to the fermentation of new ideas already growing among American painters. The stimulation of this international atmosphere was enormous for the *avant-garde* Americans. This was not so much a matter of learning or being influenced, but of difficult mutual assimilation. The McMillan Gallery exhibition organized by John Graham was a sign of the times, and when the famous Surrealist International Exhibition of 1942, with its "15 miles of string" labyrinth, opened at the Whitelaw Reid Mansion, it included two young American painters then still unknown to the larger public, William Baziotes and Robert Motherwell. Motherwell and Baziotes were germinal to these developments between the Europeans and Americans, developments, to be sure, which were not immediately realized. Motherwell, a new-comer to New York, had a characteristically articulate response to the European contribution; Baziotes, who had worked on the Federal Arts Projects, an intimate knowledge of the artists to whom this contribution might apply.

1943–47 One of the chief centers for these new developments, which were mainly International Surrealist in atmosphere, was Peggy Guggenheim's Art of This Century Gallery. Here many of the important American painters of today were first shown, and first saw recent works of their European confrères. Pollock was given his first one-man show at The Art of This Century Gallery in 1943, and a contract for his production, which continued until 1947, indicates the conviction with which Miss Guggenheim and the late Howard Putzel, her associate in the gallery, recognized Pollock's gifts. It was Robert Motherwell, again, who brought Pollock's work to their attention.

A year after his first exhibition in 1944, Pollock married Lee Krasner and they lived in New York until 1946. These years were full of activity in the New York art world, a world moving into a newly-confident consciousness of the new, burgeoning with talent, with ideas, and with possibilities. Indeed when a journal was founded in 1947 by Robert Motherwell and Harold Rosenberg to herald these ideas it was called *Possibilities.* The brilliant and influential criticisms of Clement Greenberg, Pollock's first public champion and most discerning admirer, were appearing regularly in *The Nation* during these years. Major paintings of Pollock were acquired by two public collections, the Museum of Modern Art and the San Francisco Museum of Art, although it was the contract with Peggy Guggenheim that enabled Pollock to continue painting uninterruptedly. In 1946 Jackson Pollock and his wife moved to The Springs, Easthampton, where they lived until his death.

1947–50 In 1946 two tendencies shared Pollock's attention. The one, a rather Gothic linear arabesque style, as seen in *The Blue Unconscious,* the other an all-over, rich impasto style, as in *Eyes in the Heat* and *Shimmering Substance.* This crisis was resolved in the paintings starting in 1947; the period for which he became most famous had begun.

Miss Guggenheim closed the Art of This Century Gallery and returned to Europe. Pollock continued to show every year, as he had since 1943, at the Betty Parsons Gallery, with two exhibitions in 1949 (an astonishing record of strength and fecundity). Although he was not in easy circumstances financially, the great works of this time did not fail to find their responsive audience. In 1948 Peggy Guggenheim presented works by Pollock as part of her collection in an exhibition in Venice, which was also shown in Florence, Milan, Amsterdam, Brussels and Zurich; in 1950 she organized his first one-man exhibition in Europe, which was shown in Venice and Milan. The same year Alfred H. Barr, Jr., director of collections at the Museum of Modern Art, presented Pollock in the Venice Biennale along with Gorky and de Kooning. Since then he has been included in numerous exhibitions in Europe. As early as 1948, Clement Greenberg had suggested that Pollock might well challenge John Marin and become the great American painter—now it seemed to be coming true. But Pollock was also sustaining frivolous and damaging criticisms, mostly aimed at his methods, and he received them with bitterness. He was especially vulnerable because of the personal nature of his work. It is terrible to be great alone, and the public had not yet recognized with its scorn the greatness of his American contemporaries. Where Gorky had suffered from lack of attention, Pollock suffered from attention of the wrong kind.

1951–56 Living in Easthampton, with a few painters and friends nearby and occasional *sorties* into New York to renew friendships and observe the changing milieu, Pollock continued an undiminished activity, now foraging into the black-and-white figurative period, then replenishing the resources of "all-over," "drip" and impasto paintings. It is difficult to date the works accurately, since he signed them only when they left the studio for an exhibition. In 1952 he held the first of several exhibitions at the Sidney Janis Gallery, which has continued to show work from each of his periods. Nevertheless by 1953, although several of his masterpieces are dated that year, Pollock was tortured with self-doubt and tormented by anxiety. There is, however, no torture, no self-doubt, in the beautiful paintings of these last years, and when, in his last painting *Scent,* he turned again toward his beginning and the manner of *Eyes in the Heat,* he brought to the painting a vitality and delicacy which is marvellous to behold. He died in an automobile accident on the night of August 11, 1956, and was buried in the cemetery of The Springs, Easthampton, near where he lived. The huge fieldstone near his grave bears the signature so familiar from his paintings.

His exhibition at the Museum of Modern Art, which had been planned for its "Artists in Mid-Career" Series, became a memorial exhibition.

Portrait and a Dream. 1953. Oil on canvas, 58¼ x 134⅜". Collection Lee Krasner Pollock.

SELECTED BIBLIOGRAPHY

Ashton, Dore: Review of exhibition at Janis Gallery, *Arts and Architecture,* Jan. 1956.

Barr, Alfred H., Jr.: "Gorky, de Kooning, Pollock (at the Venice Biennale)," *Art News,* June 1950.

Candee, Marjorie, ed: "Jackson Pollock," *Current Biography,* Apr. 1956.

Crispolti, E.: "Appunti su Jackson Pollock," *I 4 Soli,* Jan.-Feb. 1957.

Fitzsimmons, James: Review of exhibition at Janis Gallery, *Arts and Architecture,* Mar. 1954.

Friedman, B.H.: "Profile: Jackson Pollock," *Art in America,* Dec. 1955.

Goodnough, Robert: "Pollock Paints a Picture," *Art News,* May 1951.

Greenberg, Clement: "American-type Painting," *Partisan Review,* Spring 1955.

Greenberg, Clement: "Art" (a column), *The Nation* 1943–48, issues of Nov. 27, 1943; Apr. 7, 1945; Apr. 13, 1946; Dec. 28, 1946; Feb. 1, 1947; Jan. 24, 1948. Also comments in *Partisan Review,* No. 1, Jan.–Feb., 1952; *Harper's Bazaar* Feb. 1952; preface to Pollock Retrospective, Bennington College, 1952.

Greenberg, Clement: "The Present Prospects of American Painting and Sculpture," *Horizon,* Oct. 1947.

Greenberg, Clement: "Jackson Pollock," *Evergreen Review,* Vol. 1, No. 3, 1957.

Hess, Thomas, B.: *Abstract Painting: Background and American Phase,* New York, Viking Press, 1951.

Hunter, Sam: "Jackson Pollock: the Maze and the Minotaur," *New World Writing, Ninth Mentor Selection,* 1956.

Hunter, Sam: "Jackson Pollock" (catalog preface), the Museum of Modern Art, 1956–57.
McClure, Mike: "Ode to Jackson Pollock," *Evergreen Review,* Vol. 2, No. 6, 1958.
Guggenheim, Peggy: *Out of This Century,* New York, Dial Press, 1946.
Ossorio, Alfonso: "Jackson Pollock" (catalog preface), Betty Parsons Gallery, New York, 1951. (Reprinted in "15 Americans" catalog, the Museum of Modern Art, 1952.)
Pollock, Jackson: "Jackson Pollock," (a questionnaire), *Arts and Architecture,* Feb. 1944.
Pollock, Jackson: "My Painting," *Possibilities 1,* Winter 1947–48.
Restany, Pierre: "L'Art aux Etats-Unis: Jackson Pollock l'Eclabousseur," *Prisme des Arts,* No. 15, 1957.
Shapiro, Meyer: "The Younger American Painters of Today," *The Listener,* Jan. 26, 1956.
Sweeney, James J.: "Five American Painters," *Harper's Bazaar,* Apr. 1944.
Sweeney, James J.: "Jackson Pollock" (catalog preface), "Art of This Century" Gallery, Nov. 1943. (Also similar preface Arts Club of Chicago, Mar. 1945.)
Tyler, Parker: "Jackson Pollock: the Infinite Labyrinth," *Magazine of Art,* Mar. 1950.
Tyler, Parker: "Hopper and Pollock," *Art News Annual Christmas Edition,* 1957.
Willing, Victor: "Thoughts after a Car Crash," *Encounter* (London), Oct. 1956.

PHOTOGRAPHIC CREDITS

The photographs in this book are reproduced through the courtesy of those listed below:

Art Institute of Chicago 81
Art News 16
Oliver Baker 1, 2, 3, 4, 5, 12, 20, 28, 29, 33, 37, 40, 41, 43, 44, 45, 46, 47, 48, 53, 61, 68, 72, 73, 74, 76, 77, 78, 80, 82, 84
Ferdinand Boesch 7, 15, 27, 39, 49, 79
Rudolph Burckhardt 54, 68, 85, 86
French & Co., Inc. 22
Solomon R. Guggenheim Museum 70
Museum of Modern Art 19, 25, 26, 34, 62
Hans Namuth 21, 57, 58, 59, 66, 65
Poindexter Gallery 6
Sandak, Inc. 50
San Francisco Museum of Art 14
Soichi Sunami 8, 10, 11, 13, 17, 18, 23, 30, 31, 35, 36, 38, 42, 51, 52, 55, 63, 64, 67
Whitney Museum of American Art 56

INDEX

The roman numerals refer to text references, the *italic* numerals to the black and white plates, and the **bold face** numerals to the color plates. The titles of the reproductions are listed in *italics*.

Abstract Expressionism, 27
Action Painting, 22, 24, 27, 29
American Indians, 21, 31
Art Students League, 114
Autumn Rhythm, 14, 26, 30, **50**

Bacon, Francis, 19
Barr, Alfred H., Jr., 116
Baziotes, William, 114, 115
Benton, Thomas, 14, 15, 114
Birth, 6, 20
Black and White, Number 5, 1952, *73*
Black and White Painting, 68
Black, White and Grey, 33
Blue Poles, **1**, 22, 30, **75**
Blue Unconscious, The, 21, *22,* 115
Brooks, James, 114

Cahill, Holger, 114
Cathedral, 23, *28*
Cavallon, Giorgio, 114
Convergence, 26, **71**
Cubism, 15
Cut Out, 48

David, Jacques Louis, 16
Deep, The, 30, 31, **79**

de Kooning, Willem, 28, 29, 114, 116
Delacroix, Ferdinand Victor Eugène, 24
Drawing, 1938, 13
Drawing, before 1943, *8*
Drawing, 1950, 26, *52*
Drawing, 1952, 113
Duchamp, Marcel, 27

Easter and the Totem, 28, 31, *82*
Echo, 30, *66*
Eliot, T. S., 19
Ernst, Max, 16
Eteocles, 19
Expressionism, 23
Eyes in the Heat, 23, *24,* 115, 116
Eyes in the Heat II, 23, *29*

Federal Arts Project, 27, 28, 114, 115
Flame, The, 4
Four Opposites, 78
Frieze, 13
Full Fathom Five, 23, **27**

Gide, André, 19
Gorky, Arshile, 16, 28, 114, 116
Gothic, 17, 19

Graham, John, 114
Greenberg, Clement, 27, 28, 115, 116
Green Silver, 46
Greyed Rainbow, 81
Guardians of the Secret, 14, 18, 20, 21
Guggenheim, Peggy, 115, 116
Guston, Philips, 113, 114

Hunter, Sam, 114

Ingres, Jean Auguste Dominique, 24

Janis, Sidney, 13

Kaprow, Allan, 26
Key, The, 21, *26*
Kline, Franz, 29

Lavender Mist, 26, **53**

Magic Mirror, 9, 23
Male and Female, **7**, 17, 18
Marin, John, 116
Masson, André, 14, 15, 16
Matisse, Henri, 29, 31
Miró, Joan, 15, 16
Moon Woman Cuts the Circle, 20
Moon Vibrations, 12, *76*
Motherwell, Robert, 114, 115
Mural, 1943, *10, 11,* 14, 18
Mural, 1953, 19

Nation, The, 115
New York School, 27, 28, 29, 113
Night Ceremony, 18
Number 1, 1948, 23, 24, 25, 26, **32**
Number 5, 1948, 25, *34*
Number 14, 1948, *30*
Number 24, 1948, 24, *35*
Number 1, 1949, 24, **39**
Number 2, 1949, 26, **45**
Number 4, 1949, *38*
Number 6, 1949, *40*
Number 8, 1949, *41*
Number 10, 1949, *42*
Number 8, 1950, *55*
Number 27, 1950, *56*
Number 28, 1950, 26, *57*
Number 29, 1950, 26, 27, 29, *58*
Number 32, 1950, 14, 26, 29, *59, 60*
Number 11, 1951, 30, *64*
Number 14, 1951, 30, *65*
Number 23 ("Frogman"), 1951, *61*
Number 26, 1951, 30, *63*
Number 27, 1951, *67*
Number 6, 1952, 30, *69*
Number 12, 1952, 26, *72*

Ocean Greyness, 70
Oedipus, 19
One, 14, 26, *51*
Orozoc, José Clemente, 14
Ossorio, Alfonso, 31
Out of the Web, 26, **49**

Painting, 1948, *31*
Painting, 1951, 30, *62*
Pasiphaë, **15**, 19
Pasternak, Boris, 11
Picasso, Pablo, 11, 14, 15, 16, 17, 29
Pollock, Lee Krasner, 114, 115
Polynices, 19
Portrait and a Dream, 30, 119
Possibilities, 115
Putzel, Howard, 115

Rauschenberg, Robert, 27
Ritual, 31, *77*
Rivera, Diego, 14, 27
Romulus and Remus, 18, 21
Rosenberg, Harold, 22, 115
Rothko, Mark, 16, 114
Ryder, Albert, 114

Sabines, 18
Scent, 31, *85,* **86**, 116
Search, 31, **83**
Seascape, 2
She-Wolf, The, 13, 18
Shimmering Substance, 23, *25,* 28, 115
Siqueiros, David, Alfero, 14

Silver Square, 44
Sleeping Effort, 30, *74*
Soutine, Chaim, 31
Still, Clyfford, 16
Summertime, 24, *36*
Surrealism, 15, 17, 19

There Were Seven in Eight, 19, *21*, 31
Three, 54
Totem I, *19*, 21
Totem II, 21, *23*
Totemism, 20, 21
Tworkov, Jack, 114

Unformed Figures, 80
Untitled, ca. 1936, *3*, 12
Untitled, 1937, *5*, 13
Untitled, 1950, 13, *47*

Velasquez, Diego, 25

War, 25
White Cockatoo, 24, *37*
White Horizontal, *12*, 14
White Light, 23, *84*
White on Black I, 43
Wounded Animal, *16*, 18